MW00473601

Vanishing
Arizona

Vanishing Arizona

A young wife of an officer
of the U.S. 8th Infantry in
Apacheria during the 1870's

Martha Summerhayes

LEONAUR

Vanishing
Arizona
A young wife of an officer
of the U.S. 8th Infantry in
Apacheria during the 1870's
by Martha Summerhayes

First published under the title
Vanishing
Arizona

Leonaur is an imprint
of Oakpast Ltd

Copyright in this form © 2010 Oakpast Ltd

ISBN: 978-0-85706-134-8 (hardcover)
ISBN: 978-0-85706-133-1 (softcover)

http://www.leonaur.com

Publisher's Notes

In the interests of authenticity, the spellings, grammar and place names
used have been retained from the original editions.

The opinions of the authors represent a view of events in which she
was a participant related from her own perspective,
as such the text is relevant as an historical document.

The views expressed in this book are not necessarily
those of the publisher.

Contents

To My Son Harry Summerhayes
Who Shared the Vicissitudes
of My Life in Arizona,
This Book is Affectionately Dedicated

Preface

I have written this story of my army life at the urgent and ceaseless request of my children.

For whenever I allude to those early days, and tell to them the tales they have so often heard, they always say: "Now, mother, will you write these stories for us? Please, mother, do; we must never forget them."

Then, after an interval, "Mother, have you written those stories of Arizona yet?" until finally, with the aid of some old letters written from those very places (the letters having been preserved, with other papers of mine, by an uncle in New England long since dead), I have been able to give a fairly connected story.

I have not attempted to commemorate my husband's brave career in the Civil War, as I was not married until some years after the close of that war, nor to describe the many Indian campaigns in which he took part, nor to write about the achievements of the old Eighth Infantry. I leave all that to the historian. I have given simply the impressions made upon the mind of a young New England woman who left her comfortable home in the early seventies, to follow a second lieutenant into the wildest encampments of the American army.

Hoping the story may possess some interest for the younger women of the army, and possibly for some of our old friends, both in the army and in civil life, I venture to send it forth.

CHAPTER 1

Germany and the Army

The stalwart men of the Prussian army, the Lancers, the Dragoons, the Hussars, the clank of their sabres on the pavements, their brilliant uniforms, all made an impression upon my romantic mind, and I listened eagerly, in the quiet evenings, to tales of Hanover under King George, to stories of battles lost, and the entry of the Prussians into the old *Residenz-stadt*; the flight of the King, and the sorrow and chagrin which prevailed.

For I was living in the family of General Weste, the former *stadt-commandant* of Hanover, who had served fifty years in the army and had accompanied King George on his exit from the city. He was a gallant veteran, with the rank of General-Lieutenant, *ausser* Dienst. A charming and dignified man, accepting philosophically the fact that Hanover had become Prussian, but loyal in his heart to his King and to old Hanover; pretending great wrath when, on the King's birthday, he found yellow and white sand strewn before his door, but unable to conceal the joyful gleam in his eye when he spoke of it.

The general's wife was the daughter of a burgomaster and had been brought up in a neighbouring town. She was a dear, kind soul.

The house-keeping was simple, but stately and precise, as befitted the rank of this officer. The general was addressed by the servants as *Excellenz* and his wife as *Frau Excellenz*. A charming unmarried daughter lived at home, making, with myself, a family of four.

Life was spent quietly, and every evening, after our coffee (served in the living-room in winter, and in the garden in summer), Frau Generalin would amuse me with descriptions of life in her old home, and of how girls were brought up in her day; how industry was esteemed by her mother the greatest virtue, and idleness was punished as the most beguiling sin. She was never allowed, she said, to read, even on Sunday, without her knitting-work in her hands; and she would often sigh, and say to me, in German (for dear Frau Generalin spoke no other tongue), "*Ach*, Martha, you American girls are so differently brought up"; and I would say, "But, Frau Generalin, which way do you think is the better?"

She would then look puzzled, shrug her shoulders, and often say, "*Ach*! times are different I suppose, but my ideas can never change."

Now the dear Frau Generalin did not speak a word of English, and as I had had only a few lessons in German before I left America, I had the utmost difficulty at first in comprehending what she said. She spoke rapidly and I would listen with the closest attention, only to give up in despair, and to say, "*Gute Nacht*," evening after evening, with my head buzzing and my mind a blank.

After a few weeks, however, I began to understand everything she said, altho' I could not yet write or read the language, and I listened with the greatest interest to the story of her marriage with young Lieutenant Weste, of the bringing up of her four children, and of the old days in Hanover, before the Prussians took possession.

She described to me the brilliant Hanoverian Court, the endless festivities and balls, the stately elegance of the old city, and the cruel misfortunes of the King. And how, a few days after the King's flight, the end of all things came to her; for she was politely informed one evening, by a big Prussian major, that she must seek other lodgings—he needed her quarters. At this point she always wept, and I sympathized.

Thus I came to know military life in Germany, and I fell in

love with the army, with its brilliancy and its glitter, with its struggles and its romance, with its sharp contrasts, its deprivations, and its chivalry.

I came to know, as their guest, the best of old military society. They were very old-fashioned and precise, and Frau Generalin often told me that American girls were too *ausgelassen* in their manners. She often reproved me for seating myself upon the sofa (which was only for old people) and also for looking about too much when walking on the streets. Young girls must keep their eyes more cast down, looking up only occasionally. (I thought this dreadfully prim, as I was eager to see everything). I was expected to stop and drop a little courtesy on meeting an older woman, and then to inquire after the health of each member of the family. It seemed to take a lot of time, but all the other girls did it, and there seemed to be no hurry about anything, ever, in that elegant old *Residenz-stadt*. Surely a contrast to our bustling American towns.

A sentiment seemed to underlie everything they did. The Emperor meant so much to them, and they adored the Empress. A personal feeling, an affection, such as I had never heard of in a republic, caused me to stop and wonder if an empire were not the best, after all. And one day, when the Emperor, passing through Hanover *en route,* drove down the Georgen-strasse in an open *barouche* and raised his hat as he glanced at the sidewalk where I happened to be standing, my heart seemed to stop beating, and I was overcome by a most wonderful feeling—a feeling that in a man would have meant chivalry and loyalty unto death.

In this beautiful old city, life could not be taken any other than leisurely. Theatres with early hours, the maid coming for me with a lantern at nine o'clock, the frequent *Kaffee-klatsch*, the delightful afternoon coffee at the Georgen-garten, the visits to the Zoological gardens, where we always took our fresh rolls along with our knitting-work in a basket, and then sat at a little table in the open, and were served with coffee, sweet cream, and butter, by a strapping Hessian peasant woman—all so simple, yet

13

so elegant, so peaceful.

We heard the best music at the theatre, which was managed with the same precision, and maintained by the Government with the same generosity, as in the days of King George. No one was allowed to enter after the overture had begun, and an absolute hush prevailed.

The orchestra consisted of sixty or more pieces, and the audience was critical. The parquet was filled with officers in the gayest uniforms; there were few ladies amongst them; the latter sat mostly in the boxes, of which there were several tiers, and as soon as the curtain fell, between the acts, the officers would rise, turn around, and level their glasses at the boxes. Sometimes they came and visited in the boxes.

As I had been brought up in a town half Quaker, half Puritan, the custom of going to the theatre Sunday evenings was rather a questionable one in my mind. But I soon fell in with their ways, and found that on Sunday evenings there was always the most brilliant audience and the best plays were selected. With this break-down of the wall of narrow prejudice, I gave up others equally as narrow, and adopted the German customs with my whole heart.

I studied the language with unflinching perseverance, for this was the opportunity I had dreamed about and longed for in the barren winter evenings at Nantucket when I sat poring over Coleridge's translations of Schiller's plays and Bayard Taylor's version of Goethe's Faust.

Should I ever read these intelligently in the original?

And when my father consented for me to go over and spend a year and live in General Weste's family, there never was a happier or more grateful young woman. Appreciative and eager, I did not waste a moment, and my keen enjoyment of the German classics repaid me a hundred fold for all my industry.

Neither time nor misfortune, nor illness can take from me the memory of that year of privileges such as is given few American girls to enjoy, when they are at an age to fully appreciate them.

And so completely separated was I from the American and

English colony that I rarely heard my own language spoken, and thus I lived, ate, listened, talked, and even dreamed in German.

There seemed to be time enough to do everything we wished; and, as the Franco-Prussian war was just over (it was the year of 1871), and many troops were in garrison at Hanover, the officers could always join us at the various gardens for after-dinner coffee, which, by the way, was not taken in the *demi-tasse*, but in good generous coffee-cups, with plenty of rich cream. Every one drank at least two cups, the officers smoked, the women knitted or embroidered, and those were among the pleasantest hours I spent in Germany.

The intrusion of unwelcome visitors was never to be feared, as, by common consent, the various classes in Hanover kept by themselves, thus enjoying life much better than in a country where everybody is striving after the pleasures and luxuries enjoyed by those whom circumstances have placed above them.

The gay uniforms lent a brilliancy to every affair, however simple. Officers were not allowed to appear *en civile*, unless on leave of absence.

I used to say, "Oh, Frau General, how fascinating it all is!"

"Hush, Martha," she would say; "life in the army is not always so brilliant as it looks; in fact, we often call it, over here, 'glaenzendes Elend.'"

These bitter words made a great impression upon my mind, and in after years, on the American frontier, I seemed to hear them over and over again.

When I bade goodbye to the General and his family, I felt a tightening about my throat and my heart, and I could not speak. Life in Germany had become dear to me, and I had not known how dear until I was leaving it forever.

CHAPTER 2

I Joined the Army

I was put in charge of the captain of the North German Lloyd S. S. *Donau*, and after a most terrific cyclone in mid-ocean, in which we nearly foundered, I landed in Hoboken, sixteen days from Bremen.

My brother, Harry Dunham, met me on the pier, saying, as he took me in his arms, "You do not need to tell me what sort of a trip you have had; it is enough to look at the ship—that tells the story."

As the vessel had been about given up for lost, her arrival was somewhat of an agreeable surprise to all our friends, and to none more so than my old friend Jack, a second lieutenant of the United States army, who seemed so glad to have me back in America, that I concluded the only thing to do was to join the army myself.

A quiet wedding in the country soon followed my decision, and we set out early in April of the year 1874 to join his regiment, which was stationed at Fort Russell, Cheyenne, Wyoming Territory.

I had never been west of New York, and Cheyenne seemed to me, in contrast with the finished civilization of Europe, which I had so recently left, the wildest sort of a place.

Arriving in the morning, and alighting from the train, two gallant officers, in the uniform of the United States infantry, approached and gave us welcome; and to me, the bride, a special "welcome to the regiment" was given by each of them with outstretched hands.

Major Wilhelm said, "The ambulance is right here; you must come to our house and stay until you get your quarters."

Such was my introduction to the army—and to the army ambulance, in which I was destined to travel so many miles.

Four lively mules and a soldier driver brought us soon to the post, and Mrs. Wilhelm welcomed us to her pleasant and comfortable-looking quarters.

I had never seen an army post in America. I had always lived in places which needed no garrison, and the army, except in Germany, was an unknown quantity to me.

Fort Russell was a large post, and the garrison consisted of many companies of cavalry and infantry. It was all new and strange to me.

Soon after luncheon, Jack said to Major Wilhelm, "Well, now, I must go and look for quarters: what's the prospect?"

"You will have to turn someone out," said the Major, as they left the house together.

About an hour afterwards they returned, and Jack said, "Well, I have turned out Lynch; but," he added, "as his wife and child are away, I do not believe he'll care very much."

"Oh," said I, "I'm so sorry to have to turn anybody out!"

The major and his wife smiled, and the former remarked, "You must not have too much sympathy: it's the custom of the service—it's always done—by virtue of rank. They'll hate you for doing it, but if you don't do it they'll not respect you. After you've been turned out once yourself, you will not mind turning others out."

The following morning I drove over to Cheyenne with Mrs. Wilhelm, and as I passed Lieutenant Lynch's quarters and saw soldiers removing Mrs. Lynch's lares and penates, in the shape of a sewing machine, lamp-shades, and other home-like things, I turned away in pity that such customs could exist in our service.

To me, who had lived my life in the house in which I was born, moving was a thing to be dreaded.

But Mrs. Wilhelm comforted me, and assured me it was not such a serious matter after all. Army women were accustomed to it, she said.

CHAPTER 3

Army Housekeeping

Not knowing before I left home just what was needed for house-keeping in the army, and being able to gather only vague ideas on the subject from Jack, who declared that his quarters were furnished admirably, I had taken out with me but few articles in addition to the silver and linen-chests.

I began to have serious doubts on the subject of my *ménage*, after inspecting the bachelor furnishings which had seemed so ample to my husband. But there was so much to be seen in the way of guard mount, cavalry drill, and various military functions, besides the drives to town and the concerts of the string orchestra, that I had little time to think of the practical side of life.

Added to this, we were enjoying the delightful hospitality of the Wilhelms, and the major insisted upon making me acquainted with the "real old-fashioned army toddy" several times a day,—a new beverage to me, brought up in a blue-ribbon community, where wine-bibbing and whiskey drinking were rated as belonging to only the lowest classes. To be sure, my father always drank two fingers of fine cognac before dinner, but I had always considered that a sort of medicine for a man advanced in years.

Taken all in all, it is not to be wondered at if I saw not much in those few days besides bright buttons, blue uniforms, and shining swords.

Everything was military and gay and brilliant, and I forgot the very existence of practical things, in listening to the dreamy strains of Italian and German music, rendered by our excellent and painstaking orchestra. For the Eighth Infantry loved good music, and had imported its musicians direct from Italy.

This came to an end, however, after a few days, and I was obliged to descend from those heights to the dead level of domestic economy.

My husband informed me that the quarters were ready for our occupancy and that we could begin house-keeping at once. He had engaged a soldier named Adams for a striker; he did not know whether Adams was much of a cook, he said, but he was the only available man just then, as the companies were up north at the Agency.

Our quarters consisted of three rooms and a kitchen, which formed one-half of a double house.

I asked Jack why we could not have a whole house. I did not think I could possibly live in three rooms and a kitchen.

"Why, Martha," said he, "did you not know that women are not reckoned in at all at the War Department? A lieutenant's allowance of quarters, according to the Army Regulations, is one room and a kitchen, a captain's allowance is two rooms and a kitchen, and so on up, until a colonel has a fairly good house." I told him I thought it an outrage; that lieutenants' wives needed quite as much as colonels' wives.

He laughed and said, "You see we have already two rooms over our proper allowance; there are so many married officers, that the Government has had to stretch a point."

After indulging in some rather harsh comments upon a government which could treat lieutenants' wives so shabbily, I began to investigate my surroundings.

Jack had placed his furnishings (some lace curtains, camp chairs, and a carpet) in the living-room, and there was a forlorn-looking bedstead in the bedroom. A pine table in the dining-room and a range in the kitchen completed the outfit. A soldier had scrubbed the rough floors with a straw broom: it was absolutely forlorn, and my heart sank within me.

But then I thought of Mrs. Wilhelm's quarters, and resolved

to try my best to make ours look as cheerful and pretty as hers. A chaplain was about leaving the post and wished to dispose of his things, so we bought a carpet of him, a few more camp chairs of various designs, and a cheerful-looking table-cover. We were obliged to be very economical, as Jack was a second lieutenant, the pay was small and a little in arrears, after the wedding trip and long journey out. We bought white Holland shades for the windows, and made the three rooms fairly comfortable and then I turned my attention to the kitchen.

Jack said I should not have to buy anything at all; the Quartermaster Department furnished everything in the line of kitchen utensils; and, as his word was law, I went over to the quartermaster store-house to select the needed articles.

After what I had been told, I was surprised to find nothing smaller than two-gallon tea-kettles, meat-forks a yard long, and mess-kettles deep enough to cook rations for fifty men! I rebelled, and said I would not use such gigantic things.

My husband said: "Now, Mattie, be reasonable; all the army women keep house with these utensils; the regiment will move soon, and then what should we do with a lot of tin pans and such stuff? You know a second lieutenant is allowed only a thousand pounds of baggage when he changes station." This was a hard lesson, which I learned later.

Having been brought up in an old-time community, where women deferred to their husbands in everything, I yielded, and the huge things were sent over. I had told Mrs. Wilhelm that we were to have luncheon in our own quarters.

So Adams made a fire large enough to roast beef for a company of soldiers, and he and I attempted to boil a few eggs in the deep mess-kettle and to make the water boil in the huge tea-kettle.

But Adams, as it turned out, was not a cook, and I must confess that my own attention had been more engrossed by the study of German auxiliary verbs, during the few previous years, than with the art of cooking.

Of course, like all New England girls of that period, I knew how to make quince jelly and floating islands, but of the actual, practical side of cooking, and the management of a range, I knew nothing.

Here was a dilemma, indeed!

The eggs appeared to boil, but they did not seem to be done when we took them off, by the minute-hand of the clock.

I declared the kettle was too large; Adams said he did not understand it at all.

I could have wept with chagrin! Our first meal *a deux*!

I appealed to Jack. He said, "Why, of course, Martha, you ought to know that things do not cook as quickly at this altitude as they do down at the sea level. We are thousands of feet above the sea here in Wyoming." (I am not sure it was thousands, but it was hundreds at least.)

So that was the trouble, and I had not thought of it!

My head was giddy with the glamour, the uniform, the guard-mount, the military music, the rarefied air, the new conditions, the new interests of my life. Heine's songs, Goethe's plays, history and romance were floating through my mind. Is it to be wondered at that I and Adams together prepared the most atrocious meals that ever a new husband had to eat? I related my difficulties to Jack, and told him I thought we should never be able to manage with such kitchen utensils as were furnished by the Q. M. D.

"Oh, pshaw! You are pampered and spoiled with your New England kitchens," said he; "you will have to learn to do as other army women do—cook in cans and such things, be inventive, and learn to do with nothing." This was my first lesson in army housekeeping.

After my unpractical teacher had gone out on some official business, I ran over to Mrs. Wilhelm's quarters and said, "Will you let me see your kitchen closet?"

She assented, and I saw the most beautiful array of tin-ware, shining and neat, placed in rows upon the shelves and hanging from hooks on the wall.

"So!" I said; "my military husband does not know anything

about these things;" and I availed myself of the first trip of the ambulance over to Cheyenne, bought a stock of tinware and had it charged, and made no mention of it—because I feared that tin-ware was to be our bone of contention, and I put off the evil day.

The cooking went on better after that, but I did not have much assistance from Adams.

I had great trouble at first with the titles and the rank: but I soon learned that many of the officers were addressed by the brevet title bestowed upon them for gallant service in the Civil War, and I began to understand about the ways and customs of the army of Uncle Sam. In contrast to the Germans, the American lieutenants were not addressed by their title (except officially); I learned to "Mr." all the lieutenants who had no brevet.

One morning I suggested to Adams that he should wash the front windows; after being gone a half hour, to borrow a step-ladder, he entered the room, mounted the ladder and began. I sat writing. Suddenly, he faced around, and addressing me, said, "Madam, do you believe in spiritualism?"

"Good gracious! Adams, no; why do you ask me such a question?"

This was enough; he proceeded to give a lecture on the subject worthy of a man higher up on the ladder of this life. I bade him come to an end as soon as I dared (for I was not accustomed to soldiers), and suggested that he was forgetting his work.

It was early in April, and the snow drifted through the crevices of the old dried-out house, in banks upon our bed; but that was soon mended, and things began to go smoothly enough, when Jack was ordered to join his company, which was up at the Spotted Tail Agency.

It was expected that the Sioux under this chief would break out at any minute. They had become disaffected about some treaty. I did not like to be left alone with the Spiritualist, so Jack asked one of the laundresses, whose husband was out with the company, to come and stay and take care of me. Mrs. Patten was an old campaigner; she understood everything about officers and their ways, and she made me absolutely comfortable for those two lonely months. I always felt grateful to her; she was a dear old Irish woman.

All the families and a few officers were left at the post, and, with the daily drive to Cheyenne, some small dances and theatricals, my time was pleasantly occupied.

Cheyenne in those early days was an amusing but unattractive frontier town; it presented a great contrast to the old civilization I had so recently left. We often saw women in cotton wrappers, high-heeled slippers, and sun-bonnets, walking in the main streets. Cows, pigs, and saloons seemed to be a feature of the place.

In about six weeks, the affairs of the Sioux were settled, and the troops returned to the post. The weather began to be uncomfortably hot in those low wooden houses. I missed the comforts of home and the fresh sea air of the coast, but I tried to make the best of it.

Our sleeping-room was very small, and its one window looked out over the boundless prairie at the back of the post. On account of the great heat, we were obliged to have this window wide open at night. I heard the cries and wails of various animals, but Jack said that was nothing—they always heard them.

Once, at midnight, the wails seemed to be nearer, and I was terrified; but he told me 'twas only the half-wild cats and coyotes which prowled around the post. I asked him if they ever came in. "Gracious, no!" he said; "they are too wild."

I calmed myself for sleep—when like lightning, one of the huge creatures gave a flying leap in at our window, across the bed, and through into the living-room.

"Jerusalem!" cried the lieutenant, and flew after her, snatching his sword, which stood in the corner, and poking vigorously under the divan.

I rolled myself under the bed-covers, in the most abject terror lest she might come back the same way; and, true enough, she did, with a most piercing cry. I never had much rest after that occurrence, as we had no protection against these wild-cats.

The regiment, however, in June was ordered to Arizona, that dreaded and then unknown land, and the uncertain future was before me. I saw the other women packing china and their various belongings. I seemed to be helpless. Jack was busy with things outside. He had three large army chests, which were brought in and placed before me. "Now," he said, "all our things must go into those chests"—and I supposed they must.

I was pitifully ignorant of the details of moving, and I stood despairingly gazing into the depths of those boxes, when the jolly and stout wife of Major von Hermann passed my window. She glanced in, comprehended the situation, and entered, saying, "You do not understand how to pack? Let me help you: give me a cushion to kneel upon—now bring everything that is to be packed, and I can soon show you how to do it."

With her kind assistance the chests were packed, and I found that we had a great deal of surplus stuff which had to be put into rough cases, or rolled into packages and covered with *burlap*. Jack fumed when he saw it, and declared we could not take it all, as it exceeded our allowance of weight. I declared we must take it, or we could not exist.

With some concessions on both sides we were finally packed up, and left Fort Russell about the middle of June, with the first detachment, consisting of head-quarters and band, for San Francisco, over the Union Pacific Railroad.

For it must be remembered, that in 1874 there were no railroads in Arizona, and all troops which were sent to that distant territory either marched overland through New Mexico, or were transported by steamer from San Francisco down the coast, and up the Gulf of California to Fort Yuma, from which point they marched up the valley of the Gila to the southern posts, or continued up the Colorado River by steamer, to other points of disembarkation, whence they marched to the posts in the interior, or the northern part of the territory.

Much to my delight, we were allowed to remain over in San Francisco, and go down with the second detachment. We made the most of the time, which was about a fortnight, and on the sixth of August we embarked with six companies of soldiers, Lieutenant Colonel Wilkins in command, on the old steamship *Newbern*, Captain Metzger, for Arizona.

CHAPTER 4

Down the Pacific Coast

Now the *Newbern* was famous for being a good roller, and she lived up to her reputation. For seven days I saw only the inside of our stateroom. At the end of that time we arrived off Cape St. Lucas (the extreme southern point of Lower California), and I went on deck.

We anchored and took cattle aboard. I watched the natives tow them off, the cattle swimming behind their small boats, and then saw the poor beasts hoisted up by their horns to the deck of our ship.

I thought it most dreadfully cruel, but was informed that it had been done from time immemorial, so I ceased to talk about it, knowing that I could not reform those aged countries, and realizing, faintly perhaps (for I had never seen much of the rough side of life), that just as cruel things were done to the cattle we consume in the North.

Now that Mr. Sinclair, in his great book *The Jungle*, has brought the multiplied horrors of the great packing-houses before our very eyes, we might witness the hoisting of the cattle over the ship's side without feeling such intense pity, admitting that everything is relative, even cruelty.

It was now the middle of August, and the weather had become insufferably hot, but we were out of the long swell of the Pacific Ocean; we had rounded Cape St. Lucas, and were steaming up the Gulf of California, towards the mouth of the Great Colorado, whose red and turbulent waters empty themselves into this gulf, at its head.

I now had time to become acquainted with the officers of the regiment, whom I had not before met; they had come in from other posts and joined the command at San Francisco.

The daughter of the lieutenant-colonel was on board, the beautiful and graceful Caroline Wilkins, the *belle* of the regiment; and Major Worth, to whose company my husband belonged. I took a special interest in the latter, as I knew we must face life together in the wilds of Arizona. I had time to learn something about the regiment and its history; and that Major Worth's father, whose monument I had so often seen in New York, was the first colonel of the Eighth Infantry, when it was organized in the State of New York in 1838.

The party on board was merry enough, and even gay. There was Captain Ogilby, a great, genial Scotchman, and Captain Porter, a graduate of Dublin, and so charmingly witty. He seemed very devoted to Miss Wilkins, but Miss Wilkins was accustomed to the devotion of all the officers of the Eighth Infantry. In fact, it was said that every young lieutenant who joined the regiment had proposed to her. She was most attractive, and as she had too kind a heart to be a *coquette*, she was a universal favourite with the women as well as with the men.

There was Ella Bailey, too, Miss Wilkins' sister, with her young and handsome husband and their young baby.

Then, dear Mrs. Wilkins, who had been so many years in the army that she remembered crossing the plains in a real ox-team. She represented the best type of the older army woman—and it was so lovely to see her with her two daughters, all in the same regiment. A mother of grown-up daughters was not often met with in the army.

And Lieutenant-Colonel Wilkins, a gentleman in the truest sense of the word—a man of rather quiet tastes, never happier than when he had leisure for indulging his musical taste in strumming all sorts of Spanish *fandangos* on the guitar, or his somewhat marked talent with the pencil and brush.

The heat of the staterooms compelled us all to sleep on deck, so our mattresses were brought up by the soldiers at night, and spread about. The situation, however, was so novel and altogether ludicrous, and our fear of rats which ran about on deck so great, that sleep was well-nigh out of the question.

Before dawn, we fled to our staterooms, but by sunrise we were glad to dress and escape from their suffocating heat and go on deck again. Black coffee and hard-tack were sent up, and this sustained us until the nine-o'clock breakfast, which was elaborate, but not good. There was no milk, of course, except the heavily sweetened sort, which I could not use: it was the old-time condensed and canned milk; the meats were beyond everything, except the poor, tough, fresh beef we had seen hoisted over the side, at Cape St. Lucas. The butter, poor at the best, began to pour like oil. Black coffee and bread, and a baked sweet potato, seemed the only things that I could swallow.

The heat in the Gulf of California was intense. Our trunks were brought up from the vessel's hold, and we took out summer clothing. But how inadequate and inappropriate it was for that climate! Our faces burned and blistered; even the parting on the head burned, under the awnings which were kept spread. The ice-supply decreased alarmingly, the meats turned green, and when the steward went down into the refrigerator, which was somewhere below the quarter-deck, to get provisions for the day, every woman held a bottle of salts to her nose, and the officers fled to the forward part of the ship.

The odour which ascended from that refrigerator was indescribable: it lingered and would not go. It followed us to the table, and when we tasted the food we tasted the odour. We bribed the steward for ice. Finally, I could not go below at all, but had a baked sweet potato brought on deck, and lived several days upon that diet.

On the 14th of August we anchored off Mazatlan, a picturesque and ancient *adobe* town in old Mexico. The approach to this port was strikingly beautiful. Great rocks, cut by the surf into arches and caverns, guarded the entrance to the harbour. We anchored two miles out. A customs and a Wells-Fargo boat boarded us, and many natives came along side, bringing fresh cocoanuts, bananas, and limes. Some Mexicans bound for Guaymas came on board, and a troupe of Japanese jugglers.

While we were unloading cargo, some officers and their wives went on shore in one of the ship's boats, and found it a most interesting place. It was garrisoned by Mexican troops, uniformed in white cotton shirts and trousers. They visited the old hotel, the amphitheatre where the bull-fights were held, and the old fort. They told also about the cock-pits—and about the refreshing drinks they had.

My thirst began to be abnormal. We bought a dozen cocoanuts, and I drank the milk from them, and made up my mind to go ashore at the next port; for after nine days with only thick black coffee and bad warm water to drink, I was longing for a cup of good tea or a glass of fresh, sweet milk.

A day or so more brought us to Guaymas, another Mexican port. Mrs. Wilkins said she had heard something about an old Spaniard there, who used to cook meals for stray travellers. This was enough. I was desperately hungry and thirsty, and we decided to try and find him. Mrs. Wilkins spoke a little Spanish, and by dint of inquiries we found the man's house, a little old, forlorn, deserted-looking *adobe casa*.

We rapped vigorously upon the old door, and after some minutes a small, withered old man appeared.

Mrs. Wilkins told him what we wanted, but this ancient Delmonico declined to serve us, and said, in Spanish, the country was "a desert"; he had "nothing in the house"; he had "not cooked a meal in years"; he could not; and, finally, he would not; and he gently pushed the door to in our faces. But we did not give it up, and Mrs. Wilkins continued to persuade. I mustered what Spanish I knew, and told him I would pay him any price for a cup of coffee with fresh milk. He finally yielded, and told us to return in one hour.

So we walked around the little deserted town. I could think only of the breakfast we were to have in the old man's casa. And it met and exceeded our wildest anticipations, for, just fancy!

We were served with a delicious *boullion*, then chicken, perfectly cooked, accompanied by some dish flavoured with *chile verde*, creamy biscuit, fresh butter, and golden coffee with milk. There were three or four women and several officers in the party, and we had a merry breakfast. We paid the old man generously, thanked him warmly, and returned to the ship, fortified to endure the sight of all the green ducks that came out of the lower hold.

You must remember that the *Newbern* was a small and old propeller, not fitted up for passengers, and in those days the great refrigerating plants were unheard of. The women who go to the Philippines on our great transports of today cannot realize and will scarcely believe what we endured for lack of ice and of good food on that never-to-be-forgotten voyage down the Pacific coast and up the Gulf of California in the summer of 1874.

CHAPTER 5

The Slue

At last, after a voyage of thirteen days, we came to anchor a mile or so off Port Isabel, at the mouth of the Colorado River. A narrow but deep slue runs up into the desert land, on the east side of the river's mouth, and provides a harbour of refuge for the flat-bottomed stern-wheelers which meet the ocean steamers at this point. Hurricanes are prevalent at this season in the Gulf of California, but we had been fortunate in not meeting with any on the voyage. The wind now freshened, however, and beat the waves into angry foam, and there we lay for three days on the *Newbern*, off Port Isabel, before the sea was calm enough for the transfer of troops and baggage to the lighters.

This was excessively disagreeable. The wind was like a breath from a furnace; it seemed as though the days would never end, and the wind never stop blowing. Jack's official diary says: "One soldier died today."

Finally, on the fourth day, the wind abated, and the transfer was begun. We boarded the river steamboat *Cocopah*, towing a barge loaded with soldiers, and steamed away for the slue. I must say that we welcomed the change with delight. Towards the end of the afternoon the *Cocopah* put her nose to the shore and tied up. It seemed strange not to see pier sand docks, nor even piles to tie to. Anchors were taken ashore and the boat secured in that manner: there being no trees of sufficient size to make fast to.

The soldiers went into camp on shore. The heat down in that low, flat place was intense. Another man died that night.

What was our chagrin, the next morning, to learn that we must go back to the *Newbern*, to carry some freight from up-river. There was nothing to do but stay on board and tow that dreary barge, filled with hot, red, baked-looking ore, out to the ship, unload, and go back up the slue. Jack's diary records: *Aug. 23rd. Heat awful. Pringle died today.* He was the third soldier to succumb. It seemed to me their fate was a hard one. To die, down in that wretched place, to be rolled in a blanket and buried on those desert shores, with nothing but a heap of stones to mark their graves.

The adjutant of the battalion read the burial service, and the trumpeters stepped to the edge of the graves and sounded "Taps," which echoed sad and melancholy far over those parched and arid lands. My eyes filled with tears, for one of the soldiers was from our own company, and had been kind to me.

Jack said: "You mustn't cry, Mattie; it's a soldier's life, and when a man enlists he must take his chances."

"Yes, but," I said, "somewhere there must be a mother or sister, or someone who cares for these poor men, and it's all so sad to think of."

"Well, I know it is sad," he replied, soothingly, "but listen! It is all over, and the burial party is returning."

I listened and heard the gay strains of "The girl I left behind me," which the trumpeters were playing with all their might. "You see," said Jack, "it would not do for the soldiers to be sad when one of them dies. Why, it would demoralize the whole command. So they play these gay things to cheer them up."

And I began to feel that tears must be out of place at a soldier's funeral. I attended many a one after that, but I had too much imagination, and in spite of all my brave efforts, visions of the poor boy's mother on some little farm in Missouri or Kansas perhaps, or in some New England town, or possibly in the old country, would come before me, and my heart was filled with sadness.

The Post Hospital seemed to me a lonesome place to die in, although the surgeon and soldier attendants were kind to the sick men. There were no women nurses in the army in those days.

The next day, the *Cocopah* started again and towed a barge out to the ship. But the hot wind sprang up and blew fiercely, and we lay off and on all day, until it was calm enough to tow her back to the slue. By that time I had about given up all hope of getting any farther, and if the weather had only been cooler I could have endured with equanimity the idle life and knocking about from the ship to the slue, and from the slue to the ship. But the heat was unbearable. We had to unpack our trunks again and get out heavy-soled shoes, for the zinc which covered the decks of these river-steamers burned through the thin slippers we had worn on the ship.

That day we had a little diversion, for we saw the *Gila* come down the river and up the slue, and tie up directly alongside of us. She had on board and in barges four companies of the Twenty-third Infantry, who were going into the States. We exchanged greetings and visits, and from the great joy manifested by them all, I drew my conclusions as to what lay before us, in the dry and desolate country we were about to enter.

The women's clothes looked ridiculously old-fashioned, and I wondered if I should look that way when my time came to leave Arizona.

Little cared they, those women of the Twenty-third, for, joy upon joys! They saw the *Newbern* out there in the offing, waiting to take them back to green hills, and to cool days and nights, and to those they had left behind, three years before.

On account of the wind, which blew again with great violence, the *Cocopah* could not leave the slue that day. The officers and soldiers were desperate for something to do. So they tried fishing, and caught some "croakers," which tasted very fresh and good, after all the curried and doctored-up messes we had been obliged to eat on board ship.

We spent seven days in and out of that slue. Finally, on August the 26th, the wind subsided and we started up river. Towards sunset we arrived at a place called "Old Soldier's Camp." There the *Gila* joined us, and the command was divided between the two river-boats. We were assigned to the *Gila*, and I settled myself down with my belongings, for the remainder of the journey up river.

We resigned ourselves to the dreadful heat, and at the end of two more days the river had begun to narrow, and we arrived at Fort Yuma, which was at that time the post best known to, and most talked about by army officers of any in Arizona. No one except old campaigners knew much about any other post in the Territory.

It was said to be the very hottest place that ever existed, and from the time we left San Francisco we had heard the story, oft repeated, of the poor soldier who died at Fort Yuma, and after awhile returned to beg for his blankets, having found the regions of Pluto so much cooler than the place he had left. But the fort looked pleasant to us, as we approached. It lay on a high *mesa* to the left of us and there was a little green grass where the post was built.

None of the officers knew as yet their destination, and I found myself wishing it might be our good fortune to stay at Fort Yuma. It seemed such a friendly place.

Lieutenant Haskell, Twelfth Infantry, who was stationed there, came down to the boat to greet us, and brought us our letters from home. He then extended his gracious hospitality to us all, arranging for us to come to his quarters the next day for a meal, and dividing the party as best he could accommodate us. It fell to our lot to go to breakfast with Major and Mrs. Wells and Miss Wilkins.

An ambulance was sent the next morning, at nine o'clock, to bring us up the steep and winding road, white with heat, which led to the fort.

I can never forget the taste of the oatmeal with fresh milk, the eggs and butter, and delicious tomatoes, which were served to us in his latticed dining-room.

After twenty-three days of heat and glare, and scorching winds, and stale food, Fort Yuma and Mr. Haskell's dining-room seemed like Paradise.

Of course it was hot; it was August, and we expected it. But the heat of those places can be much alleviated by the surroundings. There were shower baths, and latticed *piazzas*, and large *ollas* hanging in the shade of them, containing cool water. Yuma was only twenty days from San Francisco, and they were able to get many things direct by steamer. Of course there was no ice, and butter was kept only by ingenious devices of the Chinese servants; there were but few vegetables, but what was to be had at all in that country, was to be had at Fort Yuma.

We staid one more day, and left two companies of the regiment there. When we departed, I felt, somehow, as though we were saying goodbye to the world and civilization, and as our boat clattered and tugged away up river with its great wheel astern, I could not help looking back longingly to old Fort Yuma.

CHAPTER 6

Up the Rio Colorado

And now began our real journey up the Colorado River, that river unknown to me except in my early geography lessons-that mighty and untamed river, which is today unknown except to the explorer, or the few people who have navigated its turbulent waters. Back in memory was the picture of it on the map; here was the reality, then, and here we were, on the steamer *Gila*, Captain Mellon, with the barge full of soldiers towing on after us, starting for Fort Mojave, some two hundred miles above.

The vague and shadowy foreboding that had fluttered through my mind before I left Fort Russell had now also become a reality and crowded out every other thought. The river, the scenery, seemed, after all, but an illusion, and interested me but in a dreamy sort of way.

We had staterooms, but could not remain in them long at a time, on account of the intense heat. I had never felt such heat, and no one else ever had or has since. The days were interminable. We wandered around the boat, first forward, then aft, to find a cool spot. We hung up our canteens (covered with flannel and dipped in water), where they would swing in the shade, thereby obtaining water which was a trifle cooler than the air. There was no ice, and consequently no fresh provisions. A Chinaman served as steward and cook, and at the ringing of a bell we all went into a small saloon back of the pilothouse, where the meals were served.

Our party at table on the *Gila* consisted of several unmarried officers, and several officers with their wives, about eight or nine in all, and we could have had a merry time enough but for the awful heat, which destroyed both our good looks and our tempers. The fare was meagre, of course; fresh biscuit without butter, very salt boiled beef, and some canned vegetables, which were poor enough in those days. Pies made from preserved peaches or plums generally followed this delectable course. Chinamen, as we all know, can make pies under conditions that would stagger most chefs. They may have no marble pastry-slab, and the lard may run like oil, still they can make pies that taste good to the hungry traveller.

But that dining-room was hot! The metal handles of the knives were uncomfortably warm to the touch; and even the wooden arms of the chairs felt as if they were slowly igniting. After a hasty meal, and a few remarks upon the salt beef, and the general misery of our lot, we would seek some spot which might be a trifle cooler. A *siesta* was out of the question, as the staterooms were insufferable; and so we dragged out the weary days.

At sundown the boat put her nose up to the bank and tied up for the night. The soldiers left the barges and went into camp on shore, to cook their suppers and to sleep. The banks of the river offered no very attractive spot upon which to make a camp; they were low, flat, and covered with underbrush and arrow-weed, which grew thick to the water's edge. I always found it interesting to watch the barge unload the men at sundown.

At twilight some of the soldiers came on board and laid our mattresses side by side on the after deck. *Pajamas* and loose gowns were soon en evidence, but nothing mattered, as they were no electric lights to disturb us with their glare. Rank also mattered not; Lieutenant-Colonel Wilkins and his wife lay down to rest, with the captains and lieutenants and their wives, wherever their respective strikers had placed their mattresses (for this was the good old time when the soldiers were allowed to wait upon officers families).

Under these circumstances, much sleep was not to be thought

of; the sultry heat by the river bank, and the pungent smell of the arrow-weed which lined the shores thickly, contributed more to stimulate than to soothe the weary nerves. But the glare of the sun was gone, and after awhile a stillness settled down upon this company of Uncle Sam's servants and their followers. (In the Army Regulations, wives are not rated except as "camp followers.")

But even this short respite from the glare of the sun was soon to end; for before the crack of dawn, or, as it seemed to us, shortly after midnight, came such a clatter with the fires and the high-pressure engine and the sparks, and what all they did in that wild and reckless land, that further rest was impossible, and we betook ourselves with our mattresses to the staterooms, for another attempt at sleep, which, however, meant only failure, as the sun rose incredibly early on that river, and we were glad to take a hasty sponge from a basin of rather thick looking river-water, and go again out on deck, where we could always get a cup of black coffee from the Chinaman.

And thus began another day of intolerable glare and heat. Conversation lagged; no topic seemed to have any interest except the thermometer, which hung in the coolest place on the boat; and one day when Major Worth looked at it and pronounced it one hundred and twenty-two in the shade, a grim despair seized upon me, and I wondered how much more heat human beings could endure. There was nothing to relieve the monotony of the scenery. On each side of us, low river banks, and nothing between those and the horizon line. On our left was Lower[1] California, and on our right, Arizona. Both appeared to be deserts.

As the river narrowed, however, the trip began to be enlivened by the constant danger of getting aground on the shifting sand-bars which are so numerous in this mighty river. Jack Mellon was then the most famous pilot on the Colorado, and he

---

1. This term is here used (as we used it at Ehrenberg) to designate the low, flat lands west of the river, without any reference to Lower California proper,—the long peninsula belonging to Mexico.

was very skilful in steering clear of the sand-bars, skimming over them, or working his boat off, when once fast upon them. The deck-hands, men of a mixed Indian and Mexican race, stood ready with long poles, in the bow, to jump overboard, when we struck a bar, and by dint of pushing, and reversing the engine, the boat would swing off.

On approaching a shallow place, they would sound with their poles, and in a sing-song high-pitched tone drawl out the number of feet. Sometimes their sleepy drawling tones would suddenly cease, and crying loudly, "No *alli agua!*" they would swing themselves over the side of the boat into the river, and begin their strange and intricate manipulations with the poles. Then, again, they would carry the anchor away off and by means of great spars, and some method too complicated for me to describe, Captain Mellon would fairly lift the boat over the bar.

But our progress was naturally much retarded, and sometimes we were aground an hour, sometimes a half day or more. Captain Mellon was always cheerful. River steamboating was his life, and sand-bars were his excitement. On one occasion, I said, "Oh! Captain, do you think we shall get off this bar today?"

"Well, you can't tell," he said, with a twinkle in his eye; "one trip, I lay fifty-two days on a bar," and then, after a short pause, "but that don't happen very often; we sometimes lay a week, though; there is no telling; the bars change all the time."

Sometimes the low trees and brushwood on the banks parted, and a young squaw would peer out at us. This was a little diversion, and picturesque besides. They wore very short skirts made of stripped bark, and as they held back the branches of the low willows, and looked at us with curiosity, they made pictures so pretty that I have never forgotten them. We had no Kodaks then, but even if we had had them, they could not have reproduced the fine copper colour of those bare shoulders and arms, the soft wood colours of the short bark skirts, the gleam of the sun upon their blue-black hair, and the turquoise color of the wide bead-bands which encircled their arms.

One morning, as I was trying to finish out a nap in my stateroom, Jack came excitedly in and said: "Get up, Martha, we are coming to Ehrenberg!" Visions of castles on the Rhine, and stories of the middle ages floated through my mind, as I sprang up, in pleasurable anticipation of seeing an interesting and beautiful place. Alas! for my ignorance. I saw but a row of low thatched hovels, perched on the edge of the ragged looking river-bank; a road ran lengthwise along, and opposite the hovels I saw a store and some more mean-looking huts of *adobe*.

"Oh! Jack!" I cried, "and is that Ehrenberg? Who on earth gave such a name to the wretched place?"

"Oh, some old German prospector, I suppose; but never mind, the place is all right enough. Come! Hurry up! We are going to stop here and land freight. There is an officer stationed here. See those low white walls? That is where he lives. Captain Bernard of the Fifth Cavalry. It's quite a place; come out and see it."

But I did not go ashore. Of all dreary, miserable-looking settlements that one could possibly imagine, that was the worst. An unfriendly, dirty, and Heaven-forsaken place, inhabited by a poor class of Mexicans and half-breeds. It was, however, an important shipping station for freight which was to be sent overland to the interior, and there was always one army officer stationed there.

Captain Bernard came on board to see us. I did not ask him how he liked his station; it seemed to me too satirical; like asking the Prisoner of Chillon, for instance, how he liked his dungeon.

I looked over towards those low white walls, which enclosed the Government corral and the habitation of this officer, and thanked my stars that no such dreadful detail had come to my husband. I did not dream that in less than a year this exceptionally hard fate was to be my own.

We left Ehrenberg with no regrets, and pushed on up river.

On the third of September the boilers "foamed" so that we had to tie up for nearly a day. This was caused by the water being so very muddy. The Rio Colorado deserves its name, for its swift-flowing current sweeps by like a mass of seething red liquid, turbulent and thick and treacherous. It was said on the river, that those who sank beneath its surface were never seen again, and in looking over into those whirlpools and swirling eddies, one might well believe this to be true.

From there on, up the river, we passed through great canons and the scenery was grand enough; but one cannot enjoy scenery with the mercury ranging from 107 to 122 in the shade. The grandeur was quite lost upon us all, and we were suffocated by the scorching heat radiating from those massive walls of rocks between which we puffed and clattered along.

I must confess that the history of this great river was quite unknown to me then. I had never read of the early attempts made to explore it, both from above and from its mouth, and the wonders of the "Grand Canon" were as yet unknown to the world. I did not realize that, as we steamed along between those high perpendicular walls of rock, we were really seeing the lower end of that great chasm which now, thirty years later, has become one of the most famous resorts of this country and, in fact, of the world.

There was some mention made of Major Powell, that daring adventurer, who, a few years previously, had accomplished the marvellous feat of going down the Colorado and through the Grand Canon, in a small boat, he being the first man who had at that time ever accomplished it, many men having lost their lives in the attempt.

At last, on the 8th of September, we arrived at Camp Mojave, on the right bank of the river; a low, square enclosure, on the low level of the flat land near the river. It seemed an age since we had left Yuma and twice an age since we had left the mouth of the river. But it was only eighteen days in all, and Captain Mellon remarked: "A quick trip!" and congratulated us on the good luck we had had in not being detained on the sandbars.

"Great Heavens," I thought, "if that is what they call a quick trip!" But I do not know just what I thought, for those eighteen days on the Great Colorado in midsummer, had burned themselves into my memory, and I made an inward vow that nothing would ever force me into such a situation again. I did not stop

42

to really think; I only felt, and my only feeling was a desire to get cool and to get out of the Territory in some other way and at some cooler season. How futile a wish, and how futile a vow!

Dellenbaugh, who was with Powell in 1869 in his second expedition down the river in small boats, has given to the world a most interesting account of this wonderful river and the canons through which it cuts its tempestuous way to the Gulf of California, in two volumes entitled *The Romance of the Great Colorado* and *A Canon Voyage.*

We bade goodbye to our gallant river captain and watched the great stern-wheeler as she swung out into the stream, and, heading up river, disappeared around a bend; for even at that time this venturesome pilot had pushed his boat farther up than any other steam-craft had ever gone, and we heard that there were terrific rapids and falls and unknown mysteries above. The superstition of centuries hovered over the "great cut," and but few civilized beings had looked down into its awful depths. Brave, dashing, handsome Jack Mellon! What would I give and what would we all give, to see thee once more, thou Wizard of the Great Colorado!

We turned our faces towards the Mojave desert, and I wondered, what next?

The Post Surgeon kindly took care of us for two days and nights, and we slept upon the broad *piazzas* of his quarters.

We heard no more the crackling and fizzing of the stern-wheeler's high-pressure engines at daylight, and our eyes, tired with gazing at the red whirlpools of the river, found relief in looking out upon the grey-white flat expanse which surrounded Fort Mojave, and merged itself into the desert beyond.

CHAPTER 7

The Mojave Desert

Thou white and dried-up sea! so old!
So strewn with wealth, so sown with gold!
Yes, thou art old and hoary white
With time and ruin of all things,
And on thy lonesome borders
Night Sits brooding o'er with drooping wings.
                                        —Joaquin Miller.

The country had grown steadily more unfriendly ever since leaving Fort Yuma, and the surroundings of Camp Mojave were dreary enough.

But we took time to sort out our belongings, and the officers arranged for transportation across the Territory. Some had bought, in San Francisco, comfortable travelling-carriages for their families. They were old campaigners; they knew a thing or two about Arizona; we lieutenants did not know, we had never heard much about this part of our country. But a comfortable large carriage, known as a Dougherty wagon, or, in common army parlance, an ambulance, was secured for me to travel in. This vehicle had a large body, with two seats facing each other, and a seat outside for the driver. The inside of the wagon could be closed if desired by canvas sides and back which rolled up and down, and by a curtain which dropped behind the driver's seat. So I was enabled to have some degree of privacy, if I wished.

We repacked our mess-chest, and bought from the Commissary at Mojave the provisions necessary for the long journey to

Fort Whipple, which was the destination of one of the companies and the headquarters officers.

On the morning of September 10th everything in the post was astir with preparations for the first march. It was now thirty-five days since we left San Francisco, but the change from boat to land travelling offered an agreeable diversion after the monotony of the river. I watched with interest the loading of the great prairie-schooners, into which went the soldiers' boxes and the camp equipage. Outside was lashed a good deal of the lighter stuff; I noticed a barrel of china, which looked much like our own, lashed directly over one wheel. Then there were the massive blue army wagons, which were also heavily loaded; the laundresses with their children and belongings were placed in these.

At last the command moved out. It was to me a novel sight. The wagons and schooners were each drawn by teams of six heavy mules, while a team of six lighter mules was put to each ambulance and carriage. These were quite different from the draught animals I had always seen in the Eastern States; these Government mules being sleek, well-fed and trained to trot as fast as the average carriage-horse. The harnesses were quite smart, being trimmed off with white ivory rings. Each mule was "Lize" or "Fanny" or "Kate", and the soldiers who handled the lines were accustomed to the work; for work, and arduous work, it proved to be, as we advanced into the then unknown Territory of Arizona.

The main body of the troops marched in advance; then came the ambulances and carriages, followed by the baggage-wagons and a small rear-guard. When the troops were halted once an hour for rest, the officers, who marched with the soldiers, would come to the ambulances and chat awhile, until the bugle call for "Assembly" sounded, when they would join their commands again, the men would fall in, the call "Forward" was sounded, and the small-sized army train moved on.

The first day's march was over a dreary country; a hot wind blew, and everything was filled with dust. I had long ago discarded my hat, as an unnecessary and troublesome article; consequently my head was now a mass of fine white dust, which stuck fast, of course. I was covered from head to foot with it, and it would not shake off, so, although our steamboat troubles were over, our land troubles had begun.

We reached, after a few hours' travel, the desolate place where we were to camp.

In the mean time, it had been arranged for Major Worth, who had no family, to share our mess, and we had secured the services of a soldier belonging to his company whose ability as a camp cook was known to both officers.

I cannot say that life in the army, as far as I had gone, presented any very great attractions. This, our first camp, was on the river, a little above Hardyville. Good water was there, and that was all; I had not yet learned to appreciate that. There was not a tree nor a shrub to give shade. The only thing I could see, except sky and sand, was a ruined adobe enclosure, with no roof. I sat in the ambulance until our tent was pitched, and then Jack came to me, followed by a six-foot soldier, and said: "Mattie, this is Bowen, our striker; now I want you to tell him what he shall cook for our supper; and—don't you think it would be nice if you could show him how to make some of those good New England doughnuts? I think Major Worth might like them; and after all the awful stuff we have had, you know," *et caetera, et caetera.*

I met the situation, after an inward struggle, and said, weakly, "Where are the eggs?"

"Oh," said he, "you don't need eggs; you're on the frontier now; you must learn to do without eggs."

Everything in me rebelled, but still I yielded. You see I had been married only six months; the women at home, and in Germany also, had always shown great deference to their husbands' wishes. But at that moment I almost wished Major Worth and Jack and Bowen and the mess-chest at the bottom of the Rio Colorado. However, I nerved myself for the effort, and when Bowen had his camp-fire made, he came and called me.

At the best, I never had much confidence in my ability as a

cook, but as a camp cook! Ah, me! Everything seemed to swim before my eyes, and I fancied that the other women were looking at me from their tents. Bowen was very civil, turned back the cover of the mess-chest and propped it up. That was the table. Then he brought me a tin basin, and some flour, some condensed milk, some sugar, and a rolling-pin, and then he hung a camp-kettle with lard in it over the fire. I stirred up a mixture in the basin, but the humiliation of failure was spared me, for just then, without warning, came one of those terrific sandstorms which prevail on the deserts of Arizona, blowing us all before it in its fury, and filling everything with sand.

We all scurried to the tents; some of them had blown down. There was not much shelter, but the storm was soon over, and we stood collecting our scattered senses. I saw Mrs. Wilkins at the door of her tent. She beckoned to me; I went over there, and she said: "Now, my dear, I am going to give you some advice. You must not take it unkindly. I am an old army woman and I have made many campaigns with the colonel; you have but just joined the army. You must never try to do any cooking at the camp-fire. The soldiers are there for that work, and they know lots more about it than any of us do."

"But, Jack," I began—

"Never mind Jack," said she; "he does not know as much as I do about it; and when you reach your post," she added, "you can show him what you can do in that line."

Bowen cleared away the sandy remains of the doubtful dough, and prepared for us a very fair supper. Soldiers' bacon, and coffee, and biscuits baked in a Dutch oven.

While waiting for the sun to set, we took a short stroll over to the *adobe* ruins. Inside the enclosure lay an enormous rattlesnake, coiled. It was the first one I had ever seen except in a cage, and I was fascinated by the horror of the round, grayish-looking heap, so near the colour of the sand on which it lay. Some soldiers came and killed it. But I noticed that Bowen took extra pains that night, to spread buffalo robes under our mattresses, and to place around them a hair *lariat*. "Snakes won't cross over that," he said, with a grin.

Bowen was a character. Originally from some farm in Vermont, he had served some years with the Eighth Infantry, and for a long time in the same company under Major Worth, and had cooked for the bachelors' mess. He was very tall, and had a good-natured face, but he did not have much opinion of what is known as etiquette, either military or civil; he seemed to consider himself a sort of protector to the officers of Company K, and now, as well, to the woman who had joined the company. He took us all under his wing, as it were, and although he had to be sharply reprimanded sometimes, in a kind of language which he seemed to expect, he was allowed more latitude than most soldiers.

This was my first night under canvas in the army. I did not like those desert places, and they grew to have a horror for me.

At four o'clock in the morning the cook's call sounded, the mules were fed, and the crunching and the braying were something to awaken the heaviest sleepers. Bowen called us. I was much upset by the dreadful dust, which was thick upon everything I touched. We had to hasten our toilet, as they were striking tents and breaking camp early, in order to reach before noon the next place where there was water. Sitting on camp-stools, around the mess-tables, in the open, before the break of day, we swallowed some black coffee and ate some rather thick slices of bacon and dry bread. The Wilkins' tent was near ours, and I said to them, rather peevishly: "Isn't this dust something awful?"

Miss Wilkins looked up with her sweet smile and gentle manner and replied: "Why, yes, Mrs. Summerhayes, it is pretty bad, but you must not worry about such a little thing as dust."

"How can I help it?" I said; "my hair, my clothes, everything full of it, and no chance for a bath or a change: a miserable little basin of water and—"

I suppose I was running on with all my grievances, but she stopped me and said again: "Soon, now, you will not mind it at all. Ella and I are army girls, you know, and we do not mind anything. There's no use in fretting about little things."

Miss Wilkins' remarks made a tremendous impression upon my mind and I began to study her philosophy.

At break of day the command marched out, their rifles on their shoulders, swaying along ahead of us, in the sunlight and the heat, which continued still to be almost unendurable. The dry white dust of this desert country boiled and surged up and around us in suffocating clouds.

I had my own canteen hung up in the ambulance, but the water in it got very warm and I learned to take but a swallow at a time, as it could not be refilled until we reached the next spring—and there is always some uncertainty in Arizona as to whether the spring or basin has gone dry. So water was precious, and we could not afford to waste a drop.

At about noon we reached a forlorn mud hut, known as Packwood's ranch. But the place had a bar, which was cheerful for some of the poor men, as the two days' marches had been rather hard upon them, being so "soft" from the long voyage. I could never begrudge a soldier a bit of cheer after the hard marches in Arizona, through miles of dust and burning heat, their canteens long emptied and their lips parched and dry. I watched them often as they marched along with their blanket-rolls, their haversacks, and their rifles, and I used to wonder that they did not complain.

About that time the greatest luxury in the entire world seemed to me to be a glass of fresh sweet milk, and I shall always remember Mr. Packwood's ranch, because we had milk to drink with our supper, and some delicious quail to eat.

Ranches in that part of Arizona meant only low *adobe* dwellings occupied by prospectors or men who kept the relays of animals for stage routes. Wretched, forbidding-looking places they were! Never a tree or a bush to give shade, never a sign of comfort or home.

Our tents were pitched near Packwood's, out in the broiling sun. They were like ovens; there was no shade, no coolness anywhere; we would have gladly slept, after the day's march, but instead we sat broiling in the ambulances, and waited for the long afternoon to wear away.

The next day dragged along in the same manner; the command marching bravely along through dust and heat and thirst, as Kipling's soldier sings:

With its best foot first
And the road a-sliding past,
An' every bloomin' campin'-ground
Exactly like the last.

Beal's Springs did not differ from the other ranch, except that possibly it was even more desolate. But a German lived there, who must have had some knowledge of cooking, for I remember that we bought a peach pie from him and ate it with a relish. I remember, too, that we gave him a good silver dollar for it.

The only other incident of that day's march was the suicide of Major Worth's pet dog "Pete." Having exhausted his ability to endure, this beautiful red setter fixed his eye upon a distant range of mountains, and ran without turning, or heeding any call, straight as the crow flies, towards them and death. We never saw him again; a ranchman told us he had known of several other instances where a well-bred dog had given up in this manner, and attempted to run for the hills. We had a large greyhound with us, but he did not desert.

Major Worth was much affected by the loss of his dog, and did not join us at supper that night. We kept a nice fat quail for him, however, and at about nine o'clock, when all was still and dark, Jack entered the Major's tent and said: "Come now, Major, my wife has sent you this nice quail; don't give up so about Pete, you know."

The major lay upon his camp-bed, with his face turned to the wall of his tent; he gave a deep sigh, rolled himself over and said: "Well, put it on the table, and light the candle; I'll try to eat it. Thank your wife for me."

So the lieutenant made a light, and lo! and behold, the plate was there, but the quail was gone! In the darkness, our great kangaroo hound had stolen noiselessly upon his master's heels, and quietly removed the bird. The two officers were dumbfounded.

Major Worth said: "D—n my luck;" and turned his face again to the wall of his tent.

Now Major Worth was just the dearest and gentlest sort of a man, but he had been born and brought up in the old army, and everyone knows that times and customs were different then.

Men drank more and swore a good deal, and while I do not wish my story to seem profane, yet I would not describe army life or the officers as I knew them, if I did not allow the latter to use an occasional strong expression.

The incident, however, served to cheer up the major, though he continued to deplore the loss of his beautiful dog.

For the next two days our route lay over the dreariest and most desolate country. It was not only dreary, it was positively hostile in its attitude towards every living thing except snakes, centipedes and spiders. They seemed to flourish in those surroundings.

Sometimes either Major Worth or Jack would come and drive along a few miles in the ambulance with me to cheer me up, and they allowed me to abuse the country to my heart's content. It seemed to do me much good. The desert was new to me then. I had not read Pierre Loti's wonderful book, *Le Desert*, and I did not see much to admire in the desolate waste lands through which we were travelling. I did not dream of the power of the desert, nor that I should ever long to see it again. But as I write, the longing possesses me, and the pictures then indelibly printed upon my mind, long forgotten amidst the scenes and events of half a lifetime, unfold themselves like a panorama before my vision and call me to come back, to look upon them once more.

CHAPTER 8

Learning How to Soldier

The grasses failed, and then a mass
Of dry red cactus ruled the land:
The sun rose right above and fell,
As falling molten from the skies,
And no winged thing was seen to pass.
                                    —Joaquin Miller.

We made fourteen miles the next day, and went into camp at a place called Freeze-wash, near some old silver mines. A bare and lonesome spot, where there was only sand to be seen, and some black, burnt-looking rocks. From under these rocks, crept great tarantulas, not forgetting lizards, snakes, and not forgetting the scorpion, which ran along with its tail turned up ready to sting anything that came in its way. The place furnished good water, however, and that was now the most important thing.

The next day's march was a long one. The guides said: "Twenty-eight miles to Willow Grove Springs."

The command halted ten minutes every hour for rest, but the sun poured down upon us, and I was glad to stay in the ambulance. It was at these times that my thoughts turned back to the East and to the blue sea and the green fields of God's country. I looked out at the men, who were getting pretty well fagged, and at the young officers whose uniforms were white with dust, and Frau Weste's words about *glaenzendes Elend* came to my mind. I fell to thinking: was the army life, then, only "glittering misery," and had I come to participate in it?

52

Some of the old soldiers had given out, and had to be put on the army wagons. I was getting to look rather fagged and seedy, and was much annoyed at my appearance. Not being acquainted with the vicissitudes of the desert, I had not brought in my travelling-case a sufficient number of thin washbodices. The few I had soon became black beyond recognition, as the dust boiled (literally) up and into the ambulance and covered me from head to foot. But there was no help for it, and no one was much better off.

It was about that time that we began to see the outlines of a great mountain away to the left and north of us. It seemed to grow nearer and nearer, and fascinated our gaze.

Willow Grove Springs was reached at four o'clock and the small cluster of willow trees was most refreshing to our tired eyes. The next day's march was over a rolling country. We began to see grass, and to feel that, at last, we were out of the desert. The wonderful mountain still loomed up large and clear on our left. I thought of the old Spanish explorers and wondered if they came so far as this, when they journeyed through that part of our country three hundred years before.

I wondered what beautiful and high-sounding name they might have given it. I wondered a good deal about that bare and isolated mountain, rising out of what seemed an endless waste of sand. I asked the driver if he knew the name of it: "That is Bill Williams' mountain, ma'am," he replied, and relapsed into his customary silence, which was unbroken except by an occasional remark to the wheelers or the leaders.

I thought of the Harz Mountains, which I had so recently tramped over, and the romantic names and legends connected with them, and I sighed to think such an imposing landmark as this should have such a prosaic name. I realized that Arizona was not a land of romance; and when Jack came to the ambulance, I said, "Don't you think it a pity that such monstrous things are allowed in America, as to call that great fine mountain 'Bill Williams' mountain'?"

"Why no," he said; "I suppose he discovered it, and I dare say he had a hard enough time before he got to it."

We camped at Fort Rock, and Lieutenant Bailey shot an antelope. It was the first game we had seen; our spirits revived a bit; the sight of green grass and trees brought new life to us.

Anvil Rock and old Camp Hualapais were our next two stopping places. We drove through groves of oaks, cedars and pines, and the days began hopefully and ended pleasantly. To be sure, the roads were very rough and our bones ached after a long day's travelling. But our tents were now pitched under tall pine trees and looked inviting. Soldiers have a knack of making a tent attractive.

"Madame, the Lieutenant's compliments, and your tent is ready."

I then alighted and found my little home awaiting me. The tent-flaps tied open, the mattresses laid, the blankets turned back, the camp-table with candle-stick upon it, and a couple of camp-chairs at the door of the tent. Surely it is good to be in the army I then thought; and after a supper consisting of soldiers' hot biscuit, antelope steak broiled over the coals, and a large cup of black coffee, I went to rest, listening to the soughing of the pines.

My mattress was spread always upon the ground, with a buffalo robe under it and a hair lariat around it, to keep off the snakes; as it is said they do not like to cross them. I found the ground more comfortable than the camp cots which were used by some of the officers, and most of the women.

The only Indians we had seen up to that time were the peaceful tribes of the Yumas, Cocopahs and Mojaves, who lived along the Colorado. We had not yet entered the land of the dread Apache.

The nights were now cool enough, and I never knew sweeter rest than came to me in the midst of those pine groves.

Our road was gradually turning southward, but for some days Bill Williams was the predominating feature of the landscape; turn whichever way we might, still this purple mountain was before us. It seemed to pervade the entire country, and took on such wonderful pink colours at sunset. Bill Williams held me in thrall, until the hills and valleys in the vicinity of Fort Whipple shut him out from my sight. But he seemed to have come into my life somehow, and in spite of his name, I loved him for the companionship he had given me during those long, hot, weary and interminable days.

About the middle of September, we arrived at American ranch, some ten miles from Fort Whipple, which was the head-quarters station. Colonel Wilkins and his family left us, and drove on to their destination. Some officers of the Fifth Cavalry rode out to greet us, and Lieutenant Earl Thomas asked me to come into the post and rest a day or two at their house, as we then had learned that K Company was to march on to Camp Apache, in the far eastern part of the Territory.

We were now enabled to get some fresh clothing from our trunks, which were in the depths of the prairie-schooners, and all the officers' wives were glad to go into the post, where we were most kindly entertained. Fort Whipple was a very gay and hospitable post, near the town of Prescott, which was the capital city of Arizona. The country being mountainous and fertile, the place was very attractive, and I felt sorry that we were not to remain there. But I soon learned that in the army, regrets were vain. I soon ceased to ask myself whether I was sorry or glad at any change in our stations.

On the next day the troops marched in, and camped outside the post. The married officers were able to join their wives, and the three days we spent there were delightful. There was a dance given, several informal dinners, drives into the town of Prescott, and festivities of various kinds. General Crook commanded the Department of Arizona then; he was out on some expedition, but Mrs. Crook gave a pleasant dinner for us. After dinner, Mrs. Crook came and sat beside me, asked kindly about our long journey, and added: "I am truly sorry the General is away; I should like for him to meet you; you are just the sort of woman he likes."

A few years afterwards I met the general, and remembering

this remark, I was conscious of making a special effort to please. The indifferent courtesy with which he treated me, however, led me to think that women are often mistaken judges of their husband's tastes.

The officers' quarters at Fort Whipple were quite commodious, and after seven weeks' continuous travelling, the comforts which surrounded me at Mrs. Thomas' home seemed like the veriest luxuries. I was much affected by the kindness shown me by people I had never met before, and I kept wondering if I should ever have an opportunity to return their courtesies. "Don't worry about that, Martha," said Jack, "your turn will come."

He proved a true prophet, for sooner or later, I saw them all again, and was able to extend to them the hospitality of an army home. Nevertheless, my heart grows warm whenever I think of the people who first welcomed me to Arizona, me a stranger in the army, and in the great southwest as well.

At Fort Whipple we met also some people we had known at Fort Russell, who had gone down with the first detachment, among them Major and Mrs. Wilhelm, who were to remain at headquarters. We bade goodbye to the colonel and his family, to the officers of F, who were to stay behind, and to our kind friends of the Fifth Cavalry.

We now made a fresh start, with Captain Ogilby in command. Two days took us into Camp Verde, which lies on a mesa above the river from which it takes its name.

Captain Brayton, of the Eight Infantry, and his wife, who were already settled at Camp Verde, received us and took the best care of us. Mrs. Brayton gave me a few more lessons in army house-keeping, and I could not have had a better teacher. I told her about Jack and the tinware; her bright eyes snapped, and she said: "Men think they know everything, but the truth is, they don't know anything; you go right ahead and have all the tinware and other things; all you can get, in fact; and when the time comes to move, send Jack out of the house, get a soldier to come in and pack you up, and say nothing about it."

"But the weight——"

"Fiddlesticks! They all say that; now you just not mind their talk, but take all you need, and it will get carried along, somehow."

Still another company left our ranks, and remained at Camp Verde. The command was now getting deplorably small, I thought, to enter an Indian country, for we were now to start for Camp Apache. Several routes were discussed, but, it being quite early in the autumn, and the Apache Indians being just then comparatively quiet, they decided to march the troops over Crook's Trail, which crossed the Mogollon range and was considered to be shorter than any other.

It was all the same to me. I had never seen a map of Arizona, and never heard of Crook's Trail. Maps never interested me, and I had not read much about life in the Territories. At that time, the history of our savage races was a blank page to me. I had been listening to the stories of an old civilization, and my mind did not adjust itself readily to the new surroundings.

CHAPTER 9

Across the Mogollons

It was a fine afternoon in the latter part of September, when our small detachment, with Captain Ogilby in command, marched out of Camp Verde. There were two companies of soldiers, numbering about a hundred men in all, five or six officers, Mrs. Bailey and myself, and a couple of laundresses. I cannot say that we were gay. Mrs. Bailey had said goodbye to her father and mother and sister at Fort Whipple, and although she was an army girl, she did not seem to bear the parting very philosophically.

Her young child, nine months old, was with her, and her husband, as stalwart and handsome an officer as ever wore shoulder-straps. But we were facing unknown dangers, in a far country, away from mother, father, sister and brother—a country infested with roving bands of the most cruel tribe ever known, who tortured before they killed. We could not even pretend to be gay.

The travelling was very difficult and rough, and both men and animals were worn out by night. But we were now in the mountains, the air was cool and pleasant, and the nights so cold that we were glad to have a small stove in our tents to dress by in the mornings. The scenery was wild and grand; in fact, beyond all that I had ever dreamed of; more than that, it seemed so untrod, so fresh, somehow, and I do not suppose that even now, in the day of railroads and tourists, many people have had the view of the Tonto Basin which we had one day from the top of the Mogollon range.

I remember thinking, as we alighted from our ambulances and stood looking over into the basin, "Surely I have never seen anything to compare with this—but oh! would any sane human being voluntarily go through with what I have endured on this journey, in order to look upon this wonderful scene?"

The roads had now become so difficult that our wagon-train could not move as fast as the lighter vehicles or the troops. Sometimes at a critical place in the road, where the ascent was not only dangerous, but doubtful, or there was, perhaps, a sharp turn, the ambulances waited to see the wagons safely over the pass. Each wagon had its six mules; each ambulance had also its quota of six.

At the foot of one of these steep places, the wagons would halt, the teamsters would inspect the road, and calculate the possibilities of reaching the top; then, furiously cracking their whips, and pouring forth volley upon volley of oaths, they would start the team. Each mule got its share of dreadful curses. I had never heard or conceived of any oaths like those. They made my blood fairly curdle, and I am not speaking figuratively. The shivers ran up and down my back, and I half expected to see those teamsters struck down by the hand of the Almighty.

For although the anathemas hurled at my innocent head, during the impressionable years of girlhood, by the pale and determined Congregational ministers with gold-bowed spectacles, who held forth in the meeting-house of my maternal ancestry (all honour to their sincerity), had taken little hold upon my mind, still, the vital drop of the Puritan was in my blood, and the fear of a personal God and His wrath still existed, away back in the hidden recesses of my heart.

This swearing and lashing went on until the heavily-loaded prairie-schooner, swaying, swinging, and swerving to the edge of the cut, and back again to the perpendicular wall of the mountain, would finally reach the top, and pass on around the bend; then another would do the same. Each teamster had his own particular variety of oaths, each mule had a feminine name, and this brought the swearing down to a sort of personal basis. I remonstrated with Jack, but he said: teamsters always swore; "the mules wouldn't even stir to go up a hill, if they weren't sworn at like that."

By the time we had crossed the great Mogollon *mesa*, I had become accustomed to those dreadful oaths, and learned to admire the skill, persistency and endurance shown by those rough teamsters. I actually got so far as to believe what Jack had told me about the swearing being necessary, for I saw impossible feats performed by the combination.

When near camp, and over the difficult places, we drove on ahead and waited for the wagons to come in. It was sometimes late evening before tents could be pitched and supper cooked. And oh! to see the poor jaded animals when the wagons reached camp! I could forget my own discomfort and even hunger, when I looked at their sad faces.

One night the teamsters reported that a six-mule team had rolled down the steep side of a mountain. I did not ask what became of the poor faithful mules; I do not know, to this day. In my pity and real distress over the fate of these patient brutes, I forgot to inquire what boxes were on the unfortunate wagon.

We began to have some shooting. Lieutenant Bailey shot a young deer, and some wild turkeys, and we could not complain any more of the lack of fresh food.

It did not surprise us to learn that ours was the first wagon-train to pass over Crook's Trail. For miles and miles the so-called road was nothing but a clearing, and we were pitched and jerked from side to side of the ambulance, as we struck large rocks or tree-stumps; in some steep places, logs were chained to the rear of the ambulance, to keep it from pitching forward onto the backs of the mules. At such places I got out and picked my way down the rocky declivity.

We now began to hear of the Apache Indians, who were always out, in either large or small bands, doing their murderous work.

One day a party of horseman tore past us at a gallop. Some of them raised their hats to us as they rushed past, and our officers recognized General Crook, but we could not, in the cloud of dust, distinguish officers from scouts. All wore the flannel shirt, handkerchief tied about the neck, and broad campaign hat.

After supper that evening, the conversation turned upon Indians in general, and Apaches in particular. We camped always at a basin, or a tank, or a hole, or a spring, or in some canon, by a creek. Always from water to water we marched. Our camp that night was in the midst of a primeval grove of tall pine trees; verily, an untrodden land. We had a big camp-fire, and sat around it until very late. There were only five or six officers, and Mrs. Bailey and myself.

The darkness and blackness of the place were uncanny. We all sat looking into the fire. Somebody said, "Injuns would not have such a big fire as that."

"No; you bet they wouldn't," was the quick reply of one of the officers.

Then followed a long pause; we all sat thinking, and gazing into the fire, which crackled and leaped into fitful blazes.

"Our figures must make a mighty good outline against that fire," remarked one of officers, nonchalantly; "I dare say those stealthy sons of Satan know exactly where we are at this minute," he added.

"Yes, you bet your life they do!" answered one of the younger men, lapsing into the frontiersman's language, from the force of his convictions.

"Look behind you at those trees, Jack," said Major Worth. "Can you see anything? No! And if there were an Apache behind each one of them, we should never know it."

We all turned and peered into the black darkness which surrounded us.

Another pause followed; the silence was weird—only the cracking of the fire was heard, and the mournful soughing of the wind in the pines.

Suddenly, a crash! We started to our feet and faced around.

"A dead branch," said someone.

Major Worth shrugged his shoulders, and turning to Jack,

said, in a low tone, "D——d if I don't believe I'm getting nervous," and saying "good night," he walked towards his tent.

No element of doubt pervaded my mind as to my own state. The weird feeling of being up in those remote mountain passes, with but a handful of soldiers against the wary Apaches, the mysterious look of those black tree-trunks, upon which flickered the uncertain light of the camp-fire now dying, and from behind each one of which I imagined a red devil might be at that moment taking aim with his deadly arrow, all inspired me with fear such as I had never before known.

In the cyclone which had overtaken our good ship in mid-Atlantic, where we lay tossing about at the mercy of the waves for thirty-six long hours, I had expected to yield my body to the dark and gruesome depths of the ocean. I had almost felt the cold arms of Death about me; but compared to the sickening dread of the cruel Apache, my fears then had been as naught. Facing the inevitable at sea, I had closed my eyes and said good-bye to Life. But in this mysterious darkness, every nerve, every sense, was keenly alive with terror.

Several of that small party around the camp-fire have gone from amongst us, but I venture to say that, of the few who are left, not one will deny that he shared in the vague apprehension which seized upon us.

Midnight found us still lingering around the dead ashes of the fire. After going to our tent, Jack saw that I was frightened. He said: "Don't worry, Martha, an Apache never was known to attack in the night," and after hearing many repetitions of this assertion, upon which I made him take his oath, I threw myself upon the bed. After our candle was out, I said: "When do they attack?"

Jack who, with the soldiers' indifference to danger, was already half asleep, replied: "Just before daylight, usually, but do not worry, I say; there aren't any Injuns in this neighbourhood. Why! Didn't you meet General Crook today? You ought to have some sense. If there'd been an Injun around here he would have cleaned him out. Now go to sleep and don't be foolish." But I was taking my first lessons in campaigning, and sleep was not so easy.

Just before dawn, as I had fallen into a light slumber, the flaps of the tent burst open, and began shaking violently to and fro. I sprang to my feet, prepared for the worst. Jack started up: "What is it?" he cried.

"It must have been the wind, I think, but it frightened me," I murmured. The lieutenant fastened the tent-flaps together, and lay down to sleep again; but my heart beat fast, and I listened for every sound.

The day gradually dawned, and with it my fears of the night were allayed. But ever after that, Jack's fatal answer, "Just before daylight," kept my eyes wide open for hours before the dawn.

CHAPTER 10

A Perilous Adventure

One fine afternoon, after a march of twenty-two miles over a rocky road, and finding our provisions low, Mr. Bailey and Jack went out to shoot wild turkeys. As they shouldered their guns and walked away. Captain Ogilby called out to them, "Do not go too far from camp."

Jack returned at sundown with a pair of fine turkeys! but Bailey failed to come in. However, as they all knew him to be an experienced woodsman, no one showed much anxiety until darkness had settled over the camp. Then they began to signal, by discharging their rifles; the officers went out in various directions, giving "halloos," and firing at intervals, but there came no sound of the missing man.

The camp was now thoroughly alarmed. This was too dangerous a place for a man to be wandering around in all night, and search-parties of soldiers were formed. Trees were burned, and the din of rifles, constantly discharged, added to the excitement. One party after another came in. They had scoured the country—and not a trace of Bailey.

The young wife sat in her tent, soothing her little child; everybody except her, gave up hope; the time dragged on; our hearts grew heavy; the sky was alight with blazing trees.

I went into Mrs. Bailey's tent. She was calm and altogether lovely, and said: "Charley can't get lost, and unless something has happened to him, he will come in."

Ella Bailey was a brave young army woman; she was an inspiration to the entire camp.

Finally, after hours of the keenest anxiety, a noise of gladsome shouts rang through the trees, and in came a party of men with the young officer on their shoulders. His friend Craig had been untiring in the search, and at last had heard a faint "halloo" in the distance, and one shot (the only cartridge poor Bailey had left).

After going over almost impassable places, they finally found him, lying at the bottom of a ravine. In the black darkness of the evening, he had walked directly over the edge of the chasm and fallen to the bottom, dislocating his ankle.

He was some miles from camp, and had used up all his ammunition except the one cartridge. He had tried in vain to walk or even crawl out of the ravine, but had finally been overcome by exhaustion and lay there helpless, in the wild vastnesses of the mountains.

A desperate situation, indeed! Some time afterwards, he told me how he felt, when he realized how poor his chances were, when he saw he had only one cartridge left and found that he had scarce strength to answer a "halloo," should he hear one. But soldiers never like to talk much about such things.

CHAPTER 11

Camp Apache

By the fourth of October we had crossed the range, and began to see something which looked like roads. Our animals were fagged to a state of exhaustion, but the travelling was now much easier and there was good grazing, and after three more long day's marches, we arrived at Camp Apache. We were now at our journey's end, after two months' continuous travelling, and I felt reasonably sure of shelter and a fireside for the winter at least. I knew that my husband's promotion was expected, but the immediate present was filled with an interest so absorbing, that a consideration of the future was out of the question.

At that time (it was the year of 1874) the officers' quarters at Camp Apache were log cabins, built near the edge of the deep canon through which the White Mountain River flows, before its junction with Black River.

We were welcomed by the officers of the Fifth Cavalry, who were stationed there. It was altogether picturesque and attractive. In addition to the row of log cabins, there were enormous stables and Government buildings, and a cutler's store. We were entertained for a day or two, and then quarters were assigned to us. The second lieutenants had rather a poor choice, as the quarters were scarce. We were assigned a half of a log cabin, which gave us one room, a small square hall, and a bare shed, the latter detached from the house, to be used for a kitchen. The room on the other side of the hall was occupied by the Post Surgeon, who was temporarily absent.

Our things were unloaded and brought to this cabin. I missed the barrel of china, and learned that it had been on the unfortunate wagon which rolled down the mountain-side. I had not attained that state of mind which came to me later in my army life. I cared then a good deal about my belongings, and the annoyance caused by the loss of our china was quite considerable. I knew there was none to be obtained at Camp Apache, as most of the merchandise came in by pack-train to that isolated place.

Mrs. Dodge, of the Twenty-third Infantry, who was about to leave the post, heard of my predicament, and offered me some china plates and cups, which she thought not worth the trouble of packing (so she said), and I was glad to accept them, and thanked her, almost with tears in my eyes.

Bowen nailed down our one carpet over the poor board floor (after having first sprinkled down a thick layer of clean straw, which he brought from the quartermaster stables). Two iron cots from the hospital were brought over, and two bed-sacks filled with fresh, sweet straw, were laid upon them; over these were laid our mattresses. Woven-wire springs were then unheard of in that country.

We untied our folding chairs, built a fire on the hearth, captured an old broken-legged wash-stand and a round table from somewhere, and that was our living-room. A pine table was found for the small hall, which was to be our dining-room, and some chairs with raw-hide seats were brought from the barracks, some shelves knocked up against one wall, to serve as sideboard. Now for the kitchen!

A cooking-stove and various things were sent over from the Q. M. store-house, and Bowen (the wonder of it!) drove in nails, and hung up my Fort Russell tin-ware, and put up shelves and stood my pans in rows, and polished the stove, and went out and stole a table somewhere (Bowen was invaluable in that way), polished the zinc under the stove, and lo! and behold, my army kitchen! Bowen was indeed a treasure; he said he would like to cook for us, for ten dollars a month.

We readily accepted this offer. There were no persons to be

obtained, in these distant places, who could do the cooking in the families of officers, so it was customary to employ a soldier; and the soldier often displayed remarkable ability in the way of cooking, in some cases, in fact, more than in the way of soldiering. They liked the little addition to their pay, if they were of frugal mind; they had also their own quiet room to sleep in, and I often thought the family life, offering as it did a contrast to the bareness and desolation of the noisy barracks, appealed to the domestic instinct, so strong in some men's natures. At all events, it was always easy in those days to get a man from the company, and they sometimes remained for years with an officer's family; in some cases attending drills and roll-calls besides.

Now came the unpacking of the chests and trunks. In our one diminutive room, and small hall, was no closet, there were no hooks on the bare walls, no place to hang things or lay things, and what to do I did not know. I was in despair; Jack came in, to find me sitting on the edge of a chest, which was half unpacked, the contents on the floor. I was very mournful, and he did not see why.

"Oh! Jack! I've nowhere to put things!"

"What things?" said this impossible man.

"Why, all our things," said I, losing my temper; "can't you see them?"

"Put them back in the chests,—and get them out as you need them," said this son of Mars, and buckled on his sword. "Do the best you can, Martha, I have to go to the barracks; be back again soon." I looked around me, and tried to solve the problem. There was no bureau, nothing; not a nook or corner where a thing might be stowed. I gazed at the motley collection of bed-linen, dust-pans, silver bottles, boot jacks, saddles, old uniforms, full dress military hats, sword-belts, riding-boots, cut glass, window-shades, lamps, work-baskets, and books, and I gave it up in despair. You see, I was not an army girl, and I did not know how to manage.

There was nothing to be done, however, but to follow Jack's advice, so I threw the boots, saddles and equipments under the bed, and laid the other things back in the chests, closed the lids and went out to take a look at the post. Towards evening, a soldier came for orders for beef, and I learned how to manage that. I was told that we bought our meats direct from the contractor; I had to state how much and what cuts I wished.

Another soldier came to bring us milk, and I asked Jack who was the milkman, and he said, blessed if he knew; I learned, afterwards, that the soldiers roped some of the wild Texas cows that were kept in one of the Government corrals, and tied them securely to keep them from kicking; then milked them, and the milk was divided up among the officers' families, according to rank. We received about a pint every night. I declared it was not enough; but I soon discovered that however much education, position and money might count in civil life, rank seemed to be the one and only thing in the army, and Jack had not much of that just then.

The question of getting settled comfortably still worried me, and after a day of two, I went over to see what Mrs. Bailey had done. To my surprise, I found her out playing tennis, her little boy asleep in the baby-carriage, which they had brought all the way from San Francisco, near the court. I joined the group, and afterwards asked her advice about the matter. She laughed kindly, and said: "Oh! you'll get used to it, and things will settle themselves. Of course it is troublesome, but you can have shelves and such things—you'll soon learn," and still smiling, she gave her ball a neat left-hander.

I concluded that my New England bringing up had been too serious, and wondered if I had made a dreadful mistake in marrying into the army, or at least in following my husband to Arizona. I debated the question with myself from all sides, and decided then and there that young army wives should stay at home with their mothers and fathers, and not go into such wild and uncouth places. I thought my decision irrevocable.

Before the two small deep windows in our room we hung some Turkey red cotton, Jack built in his spare moments a couch for me, and gradually our small quarters assumed an appearance of comfort. I turned my attention a little to social matters. We dined at Captain Montgomery's (the commanding officer's) house; his wife was a famous Washington beauty. He had more rank, consequently more rooms, than we had, and their quarters were very comfortable and attractive.

There was much that was new and interesting at the post. The Indians who lived on this reservation were the White Mountain Apaches, a fierce and cruel tribe, whose depredations and atrocities had been carried on for years, in and around, and, indeed, far away from their mountain homes. But this tribe was now under surveillance of the Government, and guarded by a strong garrison of cavalry and infantry at Camp Apache. They were divided into bands, under Chiefs Pedro, Diablo, Patone and Cibiano; they came into the post twice a week to be counted, and to receive their rations of beef, sugar, beans, and other staples, which Uncle Sam's commissary officer issued to them.

In the absence of other amusement, the officers' wives walked over to witness this rather solemn ceremony. At least, the serious expression on the faces of the Indians, as they received their rations, gave an air of solemnity to the proceeding.

Large stakes were driven into the ground; at each stake, sat or stood the leader of a band; a sort of father to his people; then the rest of them stretched out in several long lines, young bucks and old ones, squaws and *papooses*, the families together, about seventeen hundred souls in all. I used to walk up and down between the lines, with the other women, and the squaws looked at our clothes and chuckled, and made some of their inarticulate remarks to each other. The bucks looked admiringly at the white women, especially at the cavalry beauty, Mrs. Montgomery, although I thought that Chief Diablo cast a special eye at our young Mrs. Bailey, of the infantry.

Diablo was a handsome fellow. I was especially impressed by his extraordinary good looks.

This tribe was quiet at that time, only a few renegades escaping into the hills on their wild adventures: but I never felt any confidence in them and was, on the whole, rather afraid of them. The squaws were shy, and seldom came near the officers' quarters. Some of the younger girls were extremely pretty; they had delicate hands, and small feet encased in well-shaped *moccasins*. They wore short skirts made of stripped bark, which hung gracefully about their bare knees and supple limbs, and usually a sort of low-necked *camisa*, made neatly of coarse, unbleached muslin, with a band around the neck and arms, and, in cold weather a pretty blanket was wrapped around their shoulders and fastened at the breast in front.

In summer the blanket was replaced by a square of bright calico. Their coarse, black hair hung in long braids in front over each shoulder, and nearly all of them wore an even bang or fringe over the forehead. Of course hats were unheard of. The Apaches, both men and women, had not then departed from the customs of their ancestors, and still retained the extraordinary beauty and picturesqueness of their aboriginal dress. They wore sometimes a fine buckskin upper garment, and if of high standing in the tribe, necklaces of elks teeth.

The young lieutenants sometimes tried to make up to the prettiest ones, and offered them trinkets, pretty boxes of soap, beads, and small mirrors (so dear to the heart of the Indian girl), but the young maids were coy enough; it seemed to me they cared more for men of their own race.

Once or twice, I saw older squaws with horribly disfigured faces. I supposed it was the result of some ravaging disease, but I learned that it was the custom of this tribe, to cut off the noses of those women who were unfaithful to their lords. Poor creatures, they had my pity, for they were only children of Nature, after all, living close to the earth, close to the pulse of their mother. But this sort of punishment seemed to be the expression of the cruel and revengeful nature of the Apache.

CHAPTER 12

Life Amongst the Apaches

Bowen proved to be a fairly good cook, and I ventured to ask people to dinner in our little hall dining-room, a veritable box of a place. One day, feeling particularly ambitious to have my dinner a success, I made a bold attempt at oyster patties. With the confidence of youth and inexperience, I made the pastry, and it was a success; I took a can of Baltimore oysters, and did them up in a fashion that astonished myself, and when, after the soup, each guest was served with a hot oyster patty, one of the cavalry officers fairly gasped. "Oyster patty, if I'm alive! Where on earth—Bless my stars! And this at Camp Apache!"

"And by Holy Jerusalem! they are good, too," claimed Captain Reilly, and turning to Bowen, he said: "Bowen, did you make these?"

Bowen straightened himself up to his six foot two, clapped his heels together, and came to "attention," looked straight to the front, and replied: "Yes, sir."

I thought I heard Captain Reilly say in an undertone to his neighbour, "The hell he did," but I was not sure.

At that season, we got excellent wild turkeys there, and good Southdown mutton, and one could not complain of such living.

But I could never get accustomed to the wretched small space of one room and a hall; for the kitchen, being detached, could scarcely be counted in. I had been born and brought up in a spacious house, with plenty of bedrooms, closets, and an immense old-time garret. The forlorn makeshifts for closets, and the absence of all conveniences, annoyed me and added much to the difficulties of my situation.

Added to this, I soon discovered that my husband had a penchant for buying and collecting things which seemed utterly worthless to me, and only added to the number of articles to be handled and packed away. I begged him to refrain, and to remember that he was married, and that we had not the money to spend in such ways. He really did try to improve, and denied himself the taking of many an alluring share in raffles for old saddles, pistols, guns, and cow-boy's stuff, which were always being held at the cutler's store.

But an auction of condemned hospital stores was too much for him, and he came in triumphantly one day, bringing a box of antiquated dentist's instruments in his hand.

"Good gracious!" I cried, "what can you ever do with those forceps?"

"Oh! they are splendid," he said, "and they will come in mighty handy some time."

I saw that he loved tools and instruments, and I reflected, why not? There are lots of things I have a passion for, and love, just as he loves those things and I shall never say any more about it. "Only," I added, aloud, "do not expect me to pack up such trash when we come to move; you will have to look out for it yourself."

So with that spiteful remark from me, the episode of the forceps was ended, for the time at least.

As the winter came on, the isolation of the place had a rather depressing effect upon us all. The officers were engaged in their various duties: drill, courts-martial, instruction, and other military occupations. They found some diversion at "the store," where the ranchmen assembled and told frontier stories and played exciting games of poker. Jack's duties as commissary officer kept him much away from me, and I was very lonely.

The mail was brought in twice a week by a soldier on horseback. When he failed to come in at the usual time, much anxiety was manifested, and I learned that only a short time before, one of the mail-carriers had been killed by Indians and the mail destroyed. I did not wonder that on mail-day everybody came out in front of the quarters and asked: "Is the mail-carrier in?"

And nothing much was done or thought of on that day, until we saw him come jogging in, the mail-bag tied behind his saddle. Our letters were from two to three weeks old. The eastern mail came *via* Santa Fe to the terminus of the railroad, and then by stage; for in 1874, the railroads did not extend very far into the Southwest. At a certain point on the old New Mexico road, our man met the San Carlos carrier, and received the mail for Apache.

"I do not understand," I said, "how any soldier can be found to take such a dangerous detail."

"Why so?" said Jack. "They like it."

"I should think that when they got into those canons and narrow defiles, they would think of the horrible fate of their predecessor," said I.

"Perhaps they do," he answered; "but a soldier is always glad to get a detail that gives him a change from the routine of post life."

I was getting to learn about the indomitable pluck of our soldiers. They did not seem to be afraid of anything. At Camp Apache my opinion of the American soldier was formed, and it has never changed. In the long march across the Territory, they had cared for my wants and performed uncomplainingly for me services usually rendered by women. Those were before the days of lineal promotion. Officers remained with their regiments for many years. A feeling of regimental prestige held officers and men together. I began to share that feeling. I knew the names of the men in the company, and not one but was ready to do a service for the "Lieutenant's wife." "K" had long been a bachelor company; and now a young woman had joined it. I was a person to be pampered and cared for, and they knew besides that I was not long in the army.

During that winter I received many a wild turkey and other nice things for the table, from the men of the company. I learned to know and to thoroughly respect the enlisted man of the American army.

And now into the varied kaleidoscope of my army life stepped the Indian Agent. And of all unkempt, unshorn, disagreeable-looking personages who had ever stepped foot into our quarters, this was the worst.

"Heaven save us from a Government which appoints such men as that to watch over and deal with Indians," cried I, as he left the house. "Is it possible that his position here demands social recognition?" I added.

"Hush!" said the second lieutenant of K company. "It's the Interior Department that appoints the Indian Agents, and besides," he added, "it's not good taste on your part, Martha, to abuse the Government which gives us our bread and butter."

"Well, you can say what you like, and preach policy all you wish, no Government on earth can compel me to associate with such men as those!" With that assertion, I left the room, to prevent farther argument.

And I will here add that in my experience on the frontier, which extended over a long period, it was never my good fortune to meet with an Indian Agent who impressed me as being the right sort of a man to deal with those children of nature, for Indians are like children, and their intuitions are keen. They know and appreciate honesty and fair dealing, and they know a gentleman when they meet one.

The winter came on apace, but the weather was mild and pleasant. One day some officers came in and said we must go over to the "Ravine" that evening, where the Indians were going to have a rare sort of a dance.

There was no one to say to me: "Do not go," and, as we welcomed any little excitement which would relieve the monotony of our lives, we cast aside all doubts of the advisability of my going. So, after dinner, we joined the others, and sallied forth into the darkness of an Arizona night. We crossed the large parade-ground, and picked our way over a rough and pathless country, lighted only by the stars above.

Arriving at the edge of the ravine, what a scene was before us! We looked down into a natural amphitheatre, in which blazed great fires; hordes of wild Apaches darted about, while others sat on logs beating their *tom-toms*.

I was afraid, and held back, but the rest of the party descended into the ravine, and, leaning on a good strong arm, I followed. We all sat down on the great trunk of a fallen tree, and soon the dancers came into the arena.

They were entirely naked, except for the loin-cloth; their bodies were painted, and from their elbows and knees stood out bunches of feathers, giving them the appearance of huge flying creatures; jingling things were attached to their necks and arms. Upon their heads were large frames, made to resemble the branching horns of an elk, and as they danced, and bowed their heads, the horns lent them the appearance of some unknown animal, and added greatly to their height. Their feathers waved, their jingles shook, and their painted bodies twisted and turned in the light of the great fire, which roared and leaped on high. At one moment they were birds, at another animals, at the next they were demons.

The noise of the *tom-toms* and the harsh shouts of the Indians grew wilder and wilder. It was weird and terrifying. Then came a pause; the arena was cleared, and with much solemnity two wicked-looking creatures came out and performed a sort of shadow dance, brandishing knives as they glided through the intricate figures.

It was a fascinating but unearthly scene, and the setting completed the illusion. Fright deprived me of the power of thought, but in a sort of subconscious way I felt that Orpheus must have witnessed just such mad revels when he went down into Pluto's regions. Suddenly the shouts became war whoops, the demons brandished their knives madly, and nodded their branching horns; the *tom-toms* were beaten with a dreadful din, and terror seized my heart.

What if they be treacherous, and had lured our small party

down into this ravine for an ambush! The thing could well be, I thought. I saw uneasiness in the faces of the other women, and by mutual consent we got up and slowly took our departure. I barely had strength to climb up the steep side of the hollow. I was thankful to escape from its horrors.

Scarce three months after that some of the same band of Indians fired into the garrison and fled to the mountains. I remarked to Jack, that I thought we were very imprudent to go to see that dance, and he said he supposed we were. But I had never regarded life in such a light way as he seemed to.

Women usually like to talk over their trials and their wonderful adventures, and that is why I am writing this, I suppose. Men simply will not talk about such things.

The cavalry beauty seemed to look at this frontier life philosophically—what she really thought about it, I never knew. Mrs. Bailey was so much occupied by the care of her young child and various outdoor amusements, that she did not, apparently, think much about things that happened around us. At all events, she never seemed inclined to talk about them. There was no one else to talk to; the soil was strange, and the atmosphere a foreign one to me; life did not seem to be taken seriously out there, as it was back in New England, where they always loved to sit down and talk things over. I was downright lonesome for my mother and sisters.

I could not go out very much at that time, so I occupied myself a good deal with needlework.

One evening we heard firing across the canon. Jack caught up his sword, buckling on his belt as he went out. "Injuns fighting on the other side of the river," some soldier reported. Finding that it did not concern us, Jack said, "Come out into the back yard, Martha, and look over the stockade, and I think you can see across the river." So I hurried out to the stockade, but Jack, seeing that I was not tall enough, picked up an empty box that stood under the window of the room belonging to the Doctor, when, thud! fell something out onto the ground, and rolled away. I started involuntarily. It was dark in the yard. I stood stock still. "What was that?" I whispered.

"Nothing but an old Edam cheese," said this true-hearted soldier of mine. I knew it was not a cheese, but said no more. I stood up on the box, watched the firing like a man, and went quietly back into the quarters. After retiring, I said, "You might just a swell tell me now, you will have to sooner or later, what was in the box—it had a dreadful sound, as it rolled away on the ground."

"Well," said he, "if you must know, it was an Injun's head that the Doctor had saved, to take to Washington with him. It had a sort of a malformed skull or jaw-bone or something. But he left it behind—I guess it got a leetle to old for him to carry," he laughed. "Somebody told me there was a head in the yard, but I forgot all about it. Lucky thing you didn't see it, wasn't it? I suppose you'd been scared—well, I must tell the fatigue party to-morrow to take it away. Now don't let me forget it," and this soldier of many battles fell into the peaceful slumber which comes to those who know not fear.

The next day I overheard him telling Major Worth what had happened, and adding that he would roast that Doctor if he ever came back. I was seeing the rugged side of life, indeed, and getting accustomed to shocks.

Now the cavalry beauty gave a dinner. It was lovely; but in the midst of it, we perceived a sort of confusion of *moccasined* footsteps outside the dining-room. My nerves were, by this time, always on the alert. I glanced through the large door opening out into the hall, and saw a group of Indian scouts; they laid a coffee-sack down by the corner fireplace, near the front door. The commanding officer left the table hastily; the portiere was drawn.

I had heard tales of atrocious cruelties committed by a band of Indians who had escaped from the reservation and were ravaging the country around. I had heard how they maimed poor sheep and cut off the legs of cattle at the first joint, leaving them to die; how they tortured women, and burned their husbands and children before their eyes; I had heard also that the Indian scouts were out after them, with orders to bring them in, dead or alive.

The next day I learned that the ringleader's head was in the bag that I had seen, and that the others had surrendered and returned. The scouts were Apaches in the pay of the Government, and I always heard that, as long as they were serving as scouts, they showed themselves loyal and would hunt down their nearest relative.

Major Worth got tired of the monotony of a bachelor's life at Camp Apache and decided to give a dance in his quarters, and invite the chiefs. I think the other officers did not wholly approve of it, although they felt friendly enough towards them, as long as they were not causing disturbances. But to meet the savage Apache on a basis of social equality, in an officer's quarters, and to dance in a quadrille with him! Well, the limit of all things had been reached!

However, Major Worth, who was actually suffering from the ennui of frontier life in winter, and in time of peace, determined to carry out his project, so he had his quarters, which were quite spacious, cleared and decorated with evergreen boughs. From his company, he secured some men who could play the banjo and guitar, and all the officers and their wives, and the chiefs with their harems, came to this novel fete. A quadrille was formed, in which the chiefs danced opposite the officers. The squaws sat around, as they were too shy to dance. These chiefs were painted, and wore only their necklaces and the customary loin-cloth, throwing their blankets about their shoulders when they had finished dancing. I noticed again Chief Diablo's great good looks.

Conversation was carried on principally by signs and nods, and through the interpreter (a white man named Cooley). Besides, the officers had picked up many short phrases of the harsh and guttural Apache tongue.

Diablo was charmed with the young, handsome wife of one of the officers, and asked her husband how many ponies he would take for her, and Pedro asked Major Worth, if all those white squaws belonged to him.

The party passed off pleasantly enough, and was not especially subversive to discipline, although I believe it was not repeated.

Afterwards, long afterwards, when we were stationed at David's Island, New York Harbor, and Major Worth was no longer a bachelor, but a dignified married man and had gained his star in the Spanish War, we used to meet occasionally down by the barge office or taking a Fenster-promenade on Broadway, and we would always stand awhile and chat over the old days at Camp Apache in '74. Never mind how pressing our mutual engagements were, we could never forego the pleasure of talking over those wild days and contrasting them with our then present surroundings. "Shall you ever forget my party?" he said, the last time we met.

CHAPTER 13

A New Recruit

In January our little boy arrived, to share our fate and to gladden our hearts. As he was the first child born to an officer's family in Camp Apache, there was the greatest excitement. All the sheep-ranchers and cattlemen for miles around came into the post. The beneficent canteen, with its soldiers' and officers' clubrooms did not exist then. So they all gathered at the cutler's store, to celebrate events with a round of drinks. They wanted to shake hands with and congratulate the new father, after their fashion, upon the advent of the blond-haired baby. Their great hearts went out to him, and they vied with each other in doing the handsome thing by him, in a manner according to their lights, and their ideas of wishing well to a man; a manner, sometimes, alas! disastrous in its results to the man! However, by this time, I was getting used to all sides of frontier life.

I had no time to be lonely now, for I had no nurse, and the only person who was able to render me service was a laundress of the Fifth Cavalry, who came for about two hours each day, to give the baby his bath and to arrange things about the bed. I begged her to stay with me, but, of course, I knew it was impossible.

So here I was, inexperienced and helpless, alone in bed, with an infant a few days old. Dr. Loring, our excellent Post Surgeon, was both kind and skilful, but he was in poor health and expecting each day to be ordered to another station. My husband was obliged to be at the Commissary Office all day, issuing rations to .

troops and scouts, and attending to the duties of his position.

But, realizing in a measure the utter helplessness of my situation, he sent a soldier up to lead a wire cord through the thick wall at the head of my bed and out through the small yard into the kitchen. To this they attached a big cow-bell, so, by making some considerable effort to reach up and pull this wire, I could summon Bowen, that is, if Bowen happened to be there. But Bowen seemed always to be out at drill or over at the company quarters, and frequently my bell brought no response. When he did come, however, he was just as kind and just as awkward as it was possible for a great big six-foot farmer-soldier to be.

But I grew weaker and weaker with trying to be strong, and one day when Jack came in and found both the baby and myself crying, he said, man-like, "What's the matter?" I said, "I must have someone to take care of me, or we shall both die."

He seemed to realize that the situation was desperate, and mounted men were sent out immediately in all directions to find a woman.

At last, a Mexican girl was found in a wood-chopper's camp, and was brought to me. She was quite young and very ignorant and stupid, and spoke nothing but a sort of Mexican "lingo," and did not understand a word of English. But I felt that my life was saved; and Bowen fixed up a place on the couch for her to sleep, and Jack went over to the unoccupied room on the other side of the cabin and took possession of the absent doctor's bed.

I begged Jack to hunt up a Spanish dictionary, and fortunately one was found at the cutler's store, which, doubtless the cutler or his predecessor had brought into the country years before.

The girl did not know anything. I do not think she had ever been inside a *casa* before. She had washed herself in mountain streams, and did not know what basins and sponges were for. So it was of no use to point to the objects I wanted.

I propped myself up in bed and studied the dictionary, and, having some idea of the pronunciation of Latin languages, I essayed to call for warm water and various other necessary articles needed around a sick bed. Sometimes I succeeded in getting an idea through her impervious brain, but more often she would stand dazed and immovable and I would let the dictionary drop from my tired hands and fall back upon the pillow in a sweat of exhaustion. Then Bowen would be called in, and with the help of some perfunctory language and gestures on his part, this silent creature of the mountains would seem to wake up and try to understand.

And so I worried through those dreadful days—and the nights! Ah! we had better not describe them. The poor wild thing slept the sleep of death and could not hear my loudest calls nor desperate shouts.

So Jack attached a cord to her pillow, and I would tug and tug at that and pull the pillow from under her head. It was of no avail. She slept peacefully on, and it seemed to me, as I lay there staring at her, that not even Gabriel's trump would ever arouse her.

In desperation I would creep out of bed and wait upon myself and then confess to Jack and the doctor next day.

Well, we had to let the creature go, for she was of no use, and the Spanish dictionary was laid aside.

I struggled along, fighting against odds; how I ever got well at all is a wonder, when I think of all the sanitary precautions taken now-a-days with young mothers and babies. The doctor was ordered away and another one came. I had no advice or help from any one. Calomel or quinine are the only medicines I remember taking myself or giving to my child.

But to go back a little. The seventh day after the birth of the baby, a delegation of several squaws, wives of chiefs, came to pay me a formal visit. They brought me some finely woven baskets, and a beautiful *papoose*-basket or cradle, such as they carry their own babies in. This was made of the lightest wood, and covered with the finest skin of fawn, tanned with birch bark by their own hands, and embroidered in blue beads; it was their best work. I admired it, and tried to express to them my thanks.

These squaws took my baby (he was lying beside me on the bed), then, cooing and chuckling, they looked about the room, until they found a small pillow, which they laid into the basket-cradle, then put my baby in, drew the flaps together, and laced him into it; then stood it up, and laid it down, and laughed again in their gentle manner, and finally soothed him to sleep. I was quite touched by the friendliness of it all. They laid the cradle on the table and departed. Jack went out to bring Major Worth in, to see the pretty sight, and as the two entered the room, Jack pointed to the *papoose*-basket.

Major Worth tip-toed forward, and gazed into the cradle; he did not speak for some time; then, in his inimitable way, and half under his breath, he said, slowly, "Well, I'll be d—d!" This was all, but when he turned towards the bedside, and came and shook my hand, his eyes shone with a gentle and tender look.

And so was the new recruit introduced to the Captain of Company K.

And now there must be a bathtub for the baby. The cutler rummaged his entire place, to find something that might do. At last, he sent me a freshly scoured tub, that looked as if it might, at no very remote date, have contained salt mackerel marked "A One." So then, every morning at nine o'clock, our little half-window was black with the heads of the curious squaws and bucks, trying to get a glimpse of the fair baby's bath. A wonderful performance, it appeared to them.

Once a week this room, which was now a nursery combined with bedroom and living-room, was overhauled by the stalwart Bowen. The baby was put to sleep and laced securely into the *papoose*-basket. He was then carried into the kitchen, laid on the dresser, and I sat by with a book or needlework watching him, until Bowen had finished the room. On one of these occasions, I noticed a ledger lying upon one of the shelves.

I looked into it, and imagine my astonishment, when I read: *Aunt Hepsey's Muffins, Sarah's Indian Pudding*, and on another page, *Hasty's Lemon Tarts, Aunt Susan's Method of Cooking a Leg of Mutton*, and *Josie Well's Pressed Calf Liver*. Here were my own, my very own family recipes, copied into Bowen's ledger, in large illiterate characters; and on the fly-leaf, *Charles Bowen's Receipt*

Book. I burst into a good hearty laugh, almost the first one I had enjoyed since I arrived at Camp Apache.

The long-expected promotion to a first lieutenancy came at about this time. Jack was assigned to a company which was stationed at Camp MacDowell, but his departure for the new post was delayed until the spring should be more advanced and I should be able to undertake the long, rough trip with our young child.

The second week in April, my baby just nine weeks old, we began to pack up. I had gained a little in experience, to be sure, but I had lost my health and strength. I knew nothing of the care of a young infant, and depended entirely upon the advice of the Post Surgeon, who happened at that time to be a young man, much better versed in the sawing off of soldiers' legs than in the treatment of young mothers and babies.

The packing up was done under difficulties, and with much help from our faithful Bowen. It was arranged for Mrs. Bailey, who was to spend the summer with her parents at Fort Whipple, to make the trip at the same time, as our road to Camp Mac-Dowell took us through Fort Whipple. There were provided two ambulances with six mules each, two baggage-wagons, an escort of six cavalrymen fully armed, and a guide. Lieutenant Bailey was to accompany his wife on the trip.

I was genuinely sorry to part with Major Worth, but in the excitement and fatigue of breaking up our home, I had little time to think of my feelings. My young child absorbed all my time. Alas! for the ignorance of young women, thrust by circumstances into such a situation! I had miscalculated my strength, for I had never known illness in my life, and there was no one to tell me any better. I reckoned upon my superbly healthy nature to bring me through. In fact, I did not think much about it; I simply got ready and went, as soldiers do.

I heard them say that we were not to cross the Mogollon range, but were to go to the north of it, ford the Colorado Chiquito at Sunset Crossing, and so on to Camp Verde and Whipple Barracks by the Stoneman's Lake road. It sounded poetic and pretty.

Colorado Chiquito, Sunset Crossing, and Stoneman's Lake road! I thought to myself, they were prettier than any of the names I had heard in Arizona.

CHAPTER 14

A Memorable Journey

How broken plunged the steep descent!
How barren! Desolate and rent
By earthquake shock, the land lay dead,
Like some proud king in old-time slain.
An ugly skeleton, it gleamed
In burning sands. The fiery rain
Of fierce volcanoes here had sown
Its ashes. Burnt and black and seamed
With thunder-strokes and strewn
With cinders. Yea, so overthrown,
That wilder men than we had said,
On seeing this, with gathered breath,
"We come on the confines of death!
                    —Joaquin Miller.

Six good cavalrymen galloped along by our side, on the morning of April 24th, 1875, as with two ambulances, two army wagons, and a Mexican guide, we drove out of Camp Apache at a brisk trot.

The drivers were all armed, and spare rifles hung inside the ambulances. I wore a small derringer, with a narrow belt filled with cartridges. An incongruous sight, methinks now, it must have been. A young mother, pale and thin, a child of scarce three months in her arms, and a pistol belt around her waist!

I scarcely looked back at Camp Apache. We had a long day's march before us, and we looked ahead. Towards night we made camp at Cooley's ranch, and slept inside, on the floor. Cooley was interpreter and scout, and although he was a white man, he had married a young Indian girl, the daughter of one of the chiefs and was known as a squaw man. There seemed to be two Indian girls at his ranch; they were both tidy and good-looking, and they prepared us a most appetizing supper.

The ranch had spaces for windows, covered with thin unbleached muslin (or *manta*, as it is always called out there), glass windows being then too great a luxury in that remote place. There were some partitions inside the ranch, but no doors; and, of course, no floors except adobe. Several half-breed children, nearly naked, stood and gazed at us as we prepared for rest. This was interesting and picturesque from many standpoints perhaps, but it did not tend to make me sleepy. I lay gazing into the fire which was smouldering in the corner, and finally I said, in a whisper, "Jack, which girl do you think is Cooley's wife?"

"I don't know," answered this cross and tired man; and then added, "both of 'em, I guess."

Now this was too awful, but I knew he did not intend for me to ask any more questions. I had a difficult time, in those days, reconciling what I saw with what I had been taught was right, and I had to sort over my ideas and deep-rooted prejudices a good many times.

The two pretty squaws prepared a nice breakfast for us, and we set out, quite refreshed, to travel over the *malapais* (as the great lava-beds in that part of the country are called). There was no trace of a road. A few hours of this grinding and crunching over crushed lava wearied us all, and the animals found it hard pulling, although the country was level.

We crossed Silver Creek without difficulty, and arrived at Stinson's ranch, after travelling twenty-five miles, mostly *malapais*. Do not for a moment think of these ranches as farms. Some of them were deserted sheep ranches, and had only adobe walls standing in ruins. But the camp must have a name, and on the old maps of Arizona these names are still to be found. Of course, on the new railroad maps, they are absent. They were generally near a spring or a creek, consequently were chosen as camps.

Mrs. Bailey had her year-old boy, Howard, with her. We began to experience the utmost inconvenience from the lack of warm water and other things so necessary to the health and comfort of children. But we tried to make light of it all, and the two Lieutenants tried, in a man's way, to help us out. We declared we must have some clean towels for the next day, so we tried to rinse out, in the cold, hard water of the well, those which we had with us, and, as it was now nightfall and there was no fire inside this apparently deserted ranch, the two Lieutenants stood and held the wet towels before the camp-fire until they were dry.

Mrs. Bailey and I, too tired to move, sat and watched them and had each our own thoughts. She was an army girl and perhaps had seen such things before, but it was a situation that did not seem quite in keeping with my ideas of the fitness of things in general, and with the uniform in particular. The uniform, associated in my mind with brilliant functions, guard-mount, parades and full-dress weddings—the uniform, in fact, that I adored. As I sat, gazing at them, they both turned around, and, realizing how almost ludicrous they looked, they began to laugh. Whereupon we all four laughed and Jack said: "Nice work for United States officers! hey, Bailey?"

"It might be worse," sighed the handsome, blond-haired Bailey.

Thirty miles the next day, over a good road, brought us to Walker's ranch, on the site of old Camp Supply. This ranch was habitable in a way, and the owner said we might use the bedrooms; but the wild-cats about the place were so numerous and so troublesome in the night, that we could not sleep. I have mentioned the absence of windows in these ranches; we were now to experience the great inconvenience resulting therefrom, for the low open spaces furnished great opportunity for the cats. In at one opening, and out at another they flew, first across the Bailey's bed, then over ours. The dogs caught the spirit of the chase, and added their noise to that of the cats. Both babies began to cry, and then up got Bailey and threw his heavy campaign boots at the cats, with some fitting remarks.

A momentary silence reigned, and we tried again to sleep. Back came the cats, and then came Jack's turn with boots and travelling satchels. It was all of no avail, and we resigned ourselves. Cruelly tired, here we were, we two women, compelled to sit on hard boxes or the edge of a bed, to quiet our poor babies, all through that night, at that old sheep-ranch. Like the wretched emigrant, differing only from her inasmuch as she, never having known comfort perhaps, cannot realize her misery.

The two lieutenants slipped on their blouses, and sat looking helplessly at us, waging war on the cats at intervals. And so the dawn found us, our nerves at a tension, and our strength gone—a poor preparation for the trying day which was to follow.

We were able to buy a couple of sheep there, to take with us for supplies, and some antelope meat. We could not indulge, in foolish scruples, but I tried not to look when they tied the live sheep and threw them into one of the wagons.

Quite early in the day, we met a man who said he had been fired upon by some Indians at Sanford's Pass. We thought perhaps he had been scared by some stray shot, and we did not pay much attention to his story.

Soon after, however, we passed a sort of old *adobe* ruin, out of which crept two bare-headed Mexicans, so badly frightened that their dark faces were pallid; their hair seemed standing on end, and they looked stark mad with fear. They talked wildly to the guide, and gesticulated, pointing in the direction of the Pass. They had been fired at, and their ponies taken by some roving Apaches. They had been in hiding for over a day, and were hungry and miserable. We gave them food and drink. They implored us, by the Holy Virgin, not to go through the Pass.

What was to be done? The officers took counsel; the men looked to their arms. It was decided to go through. Jack examined his revolver, and saw that my pistol was loaded. I was instructed minutely what to do, in case we were attacked.

For miles we strained our eyes, looking in the direction whence these men had come.

At last, in mid-afternoon, we approached the Pass, a narrow defile winding down between high hills from this table-land to the plain below. To say that we feared an ambush, would not perhaps convey a very clear idea of how I felt on entering the Pass.

There was not a word spoken. I obeyed orders, and lay down in the bottom of the ambulance; I took my derringer out of the holster and cocked it. I looked at my little boy lying help-less there beside me, and at his delicate temples, lined with thin blue veins, and wondered if I could follow out the instructions I had received: for Jack had said, after the decision was made, to go through the Pass, "Now, Mattie, I don't think for a minute that there are any Injuns in that Pass, and you must not be afraid. We have got to go through it any way; but"—he hesitated,— "we may be mistaken; there may be a few of them in there, and they'll have a mighty good chance to get in a shot or two.

"And now listen: if I'm hit, you'll know what to do. You have your derringer; and when you see that there is no help for it, if they get away with the whole outfit, why, there's only one thing to be done. Don't let them get the baby, for they will carry you both off and—well, you know the squaws are much more cruel than the bucks. Don't let them get either of you alive. Now"— to the driver—"go on."

Jack was a man of few words, and seldom spoke much in times like that.

So I lay very quiet in the bottom of the ambulance. I realized that we were in great danger. My thoughts flew back to the East, and I saw, as in a flash, my father and mother, sisters and brother; I think I tried to say a short prayer for them, and that they might never know the worst. I fixed my eyes upon my husband's face. There he sat, rifle in hand, his features motionless, his eyes keenly watching out from one side of the ambulance, while a stalwart cavalry-man, carbine in hand, watched the other side of the narrow defile. The minutes seemed like hours.

The driver kept his animals steady, and we rattled along.

At last, as I perceived the steep slope of the road, I looked out, and saw that the Pass was widening out, and we must be nearing the end of it. "Keep still," said Jack, without moving a feature.

My heart seemed then to stop beating, and I dared not move again, until I heard him say, "Thank God, we're out of it! Get up, Mattie! See the river yonder? We'll cross that tonight, and then we'll be out of their God d——d country!"

This was Jack's way of working off his excitement, and I did not mind it. I knew he was not afraid of Apaches for himself, but for his wife and child. And if I had been a man, I should have said just as much and perhaps more.

We were now down in a flat country, and low alkali plains lay between us and the river. My nerves gradually recovered from the tension in which they had been held; the driver stopped his team for a moment, the other ambulance drove up alongside of us, and Ella Bailey and I looked at each other; we did not talk any, but I believe we cried just a little. Then Mr. Bailey and Jack (thinking we were giving way, I suppose) pulled out their big flasks, and we had to take a cup of good whiskey, weakened up with a little water from our canteens, which had been filled at Walker's ranch in the morning. Great Heavens! I thought, was it this morning that we left Walker's ranch, or was it a year ago? So much had I lived through in a few hours.

CHAPTER 15

Fording the Little Colorado

At a bend in the road the Mexican guide galloped up near the ambulance, and pointing off to the westward with a graceful gesture, said: "*Colorado Chiquito! Colorado Chiquito!*" And, sure enough, there in the afternoon sun lay the narrow winding river, its surface as smooth as glass, and its banks as if covered with snow.

We drove straight for the ford, known as Sunset Crossing. The guide was sure he knew the place. But the river was high, and I could not see how anybody could cross it without a boat. The Mexican rode his pony in once or twice; shook his head, and said in Spanish, "there was much quicksand. The old ford had changed much since he saw it." He galloped excitedly to and fro, along the bank of the river, always returning to the same place, and declaring "it was the ford; there was no other; he knew it well."

But the wagons not having yet arrived, it was decided not to attempt crossing until morning, when we could get a fresh start.

The sun was gradually sinking in the west, but the heat down in that alkali river-bottom even at that early season of the year was most uncomfortable. I was worn out with fright and fatigue; my poor child cried piteously and incessantly. Nothing was of any avail to soothe him. After the tents were pitched and the camp-fires made, some warm water was brought, and I tried to wash away some of the dust from him, but the alkali water only irritated his delicate skin, and his head, where it had lain on my arm, was inflamed by the constant rubbing. It began to break out in ugly blisters; I was in despair. We were about as wretchedly off as two human beings could be, and live, it seemed to me. The disappointment at not getting across the river, combined with the fear that the Indians were still in the neighbourhood, added to my nervousness and produced an exhaustion which, under other circumstances, would have meant collapse.

The mournful and demoniacal cries of the coyotes filled the night; they seemed to come close to the tent, and their number seemed to be legion. I lay with eyes wide open, watching for the day to come, and resolving each minute that if I ever escaped alive from that lonely river-bottom with its burning alkali, and its millions of howling coyotes, I would never, never risk being placed in such a situation again.

At dawn everybody got up and dressed. I looked in my small hand-mirror, and it seemed to me my hair had turned a greyish colour, and while it was not exactly white, the warm chestnut tinge never came back into it, after that day and night of terror. My eyes looked back at me large and hollow from the small glass, and I was in that state when it is easy to imagine the look of Death in one's own face. I think sometimes it comes, after we have thought ourselves near the borders. And I surely had been close to them the day before.

If perchance any of my readers have followed this narrative so far, and there be among them possibly any men, young or old, I would say to such ones: "Desist!" For what I am going to tell about in this chapter, and possibly another, concerns nobody but women, and my story will now, for awhile, not concern itself with the Eighth Foot, nor the army, nor the War Department, nor the Interior Department, nor the strategic value of Sunset Crossing, which may now be a railroad station, for all I know. It is simply a story of my journey from the far bank of the Little Colorado to Fort Whipple, and then on, by a change of orders, over mountains and valleys, cactus plains and desert lands, to the banks of the Great Colorado.

My attitude towards the places I travelled through was naturally influenced by the fact that I had a young baby in my arms the entire way, and that I was not able to endure hardship at that time. For usually, be it remembered, at that period of a child's life, both mother and infant are not out of the hands of the doctor and trained nurse, to say nothing of the assistance so gladly rendered by those near and dear.

The morning of the 28th of April dawned shortly after midnight, as mornings in Arizona generally do at that season, and after a hasty camp breakfast, and a good deal of reconnoitring on the part of the officers, who did not seem to be exactly satisfied about the Mexican's knowledge of the ford, they told him to push his pony in, and cross if he could.

He managed to pick his way across and back, after a good deal of floundering, and we decided to try the ford. First they hitched up ten mules to one of the heavily loaded baggage-wagons, the teamster cracked his whip, and in they went. But the quicksand frightened the leaders, and they lost their courage. Now when a mule loses courage, in the water, he puts his head down and is done for. The leaders disappeared entirely, then the next two and finally the whole ten of them were gone, irrevocably, as I thought.

But like a flash, the officers shouted: "Cut away those mules! Jump in there!" and amid other expletives the men plunged in, and feeling around under the water cut the poor animals loose and they began to crawl out on the other bank. I drew a long breath, for I thought the ten mules were drowned.

The guide picked his way over again to the other side and caught them up, and then I began to wonder how on earth we should ever get across.

There lay the heavy army wagon, deep mired in the middle of the stream, and what did I see? Our army chests, floating away down the river. I cried out: "Oh! do save our chests!" "They're all right, we'll get them presently," said Jack. It seemed a long time to me, before the soldiers could get them to the bank, which they did, with the aid of stout ropes. All our worldly goods were in those chests, and I knew they were soaked wet and probably ruined; but, after all, what did it matter, in the face of the serious problem which confronted us?

In the meantime, some of the men had floated the other boxes and trunks out of the wagon back to the shore, and were busy taking the huge vehicle apart. Anyone who knows the size of an army wagon will realize that this was hard work, especially as the wagon was mired, and nearly submerged. But the men worked desperately, and at last succeeded in getting every part of it back onto the dry land.

Somebody stirred up the camp-fire and put the kettle on, and Mrs. Bailey and I mixed up a smoking strong hot toddy for those brave fellows, who were by this time well exhausted. Then they set to work to make a boat, by drawing a large canvas under the body of the wagon, and fastening it securely. For this Lieutenant of mine had been a sailor-man and knew well how to meet emergencies.

One or two of the soldiers had now forded the stream on horseback, and taken over a heavy rope, which was made fast to our improvised boat. I was acquainted with all kinds of boats, from a catamaran to a full-rigged ship, but never a craft like this had I seen. Over the sides we clambered, however, and were ferried across the treacherous and glassy waters of the Little Colorado. All the baggage and the two ambulances were ferried over, and the other wagon was unloaded and drawn over by means of ropes.

This proceeding took all day, and of course we could get no farther, and were again obliged to camp in that most uncomfortable river-bottom. But we felt safer on that side. I looked at the smooth surface of the river, and its alkali shores, and the picture became indelibly impressed upon my memory. The unpleasant reality destroyed any poetic associations which might otherwise have clung to the name of Sunset Crossing in my ever vivid imagination.

After the tents were pitched, and the camp snugged up, Mr. Bailey produced some champagne and we wished each other joy, that we had made the dangerous crossing and escaped the perils of Sanford's Pass. I am afraid the champagne was not as cold as might have been desired, but the bottle had been wrapped in a wet blanket, and cooled a little in that way, and we drank it with zest, from a mess-cup.

CHAPTER 16

Stoneman's Lake

The road began now to ascend, and after twenty miles' travelling we reached a place called Updyke's Tanks. It was a nice place, with plenty of wood and grass. The next day we camped at Jay Coxe's Tanks. It was a hard day's march, and I was tired out when we arrived there. The ambulance was simply jerked over those miles of fearful rocks; one could not say driven or dragged over, for we were pitched from rock to rock the entire distance.

Stoneman's Lake Road was famous, as I afterwards heard. Perhaps it was just as well for me that I did not know about it in advance.

The sure-footed mules picked their way over these sharp-edged rocks. There was not a moment's respite. We asked a soldier to help with holding the baby, for my arms gave out entirely, and were as if paralyzed. The jolting threw us all by turns against the sides of the ambulance (which was not padded), and we all got some rather bad bruises. We finally bethought ourselves of the *papoose* basket, which we had brought along in the ambulance, having at the last moment no other place to put it. So a halt was called, we placed the tired baby in this semi-cradle, laced the sides snugly over him, and were thus enabled to carry him over those dreadful roads without danger.

He did not cry much, but the dust made him thirsty. I could not give him nourishment without stopping the entire train of wagons, on account of the constant pitching of the ambulance; delay was not advisable or expedient, so my poor little son had to endure with the rest of us. The big Alsatian cavalryman held the cradle easily in his strong arms, and so the long miles were travelled, one by one.

At noon of this day we made a refreshing halt, built a fire and took some luncheon. We found a shady, grassy spot, upon which the blankets were spread, and we stretched ourselves out upon them and rested. But we were still some miles from water, so after a short respite we were compelled to push on. We had been getting steadily higher since leaving Sunset Crossing, and now it began to be cold and looked like snow. Mrs. Bailey and I found it very trying to meet these changes of temperature. A good place for the camp was found at Coxe's Tanks, trenches were dug around the tents, and the earth banked up to keep us warm. The cool air, our great fatigue, and the comparative absence of danger combined to give us a heavenly night's rest.

Towards sunset of the next day, which was May Day, our cavalcade reached Stoneman's Lake. We had had another rough march, and had reached the limit of endurance, or thought we had, when we emerged from a mountain pass and drew rein upon the high green *mesa* overlooking Stoneman's Lake, a beautiful blue sheet of water lying there away below us. It was good to our tired eyes, which had gazed upon nothing but burnt rocks and alkali plains for so many days. Our camp was beautiful beyond description, and lay near the edge of the *mesa*, whence we could look down upon the lovely lake.

It was a complete surprise to us, as points of scenery were not much known or talked about then in Arizona. Ponds and lakes were unheard of. They did not seem to exist in that drear land of arid wastes. We never heard of water except that of the Colorado or the Gila or the tanks and basins, and irrigation ditches of the settlers. But here was a real Italian lake, a lake as blue as the skies above us. We feasted our eyes and our very souls upon it.

Bailey and the guide shot some wild turkeys, and as we had already eaten all the mutton we had along, the ragout of turkey made by the soldier-cook for our supper tasted better to us tired and hungry travellers, perhaps, than a canvasback at Delmonico's tastes to the weary lounger or the over-worked financier.

In the course of the day, we had passed a sort of sign-board, with the rudely written inscription, "Camp Starvation," and we had heard from Mr. Bailey the story of the tragic misfortunes at this very place of the well-known Hitchcock family of Arizona. The road was lined with dry bones, and skulls of oxen, white and bleached in the sun, lying on the bare rocks. Indeed, at every stage of the road we had seen evidences of hard travel, exhausted cattle, anxious teamsters, hunger and thirst, despair, starvation, and death.

However, Stoneman's Lake remains a joy in the memory, and far and away the most beautiful spot I ever saw in Arizona. But unless the approaches to it are made easier, tourists will never gaze upon it.

In the distance we saw the "divide," over which we must pass in order to reach Camp Verde, which was to be our first stopping place, and we looked joyfully towards the next day's march, which we expected would bring us there.

We thought the worst was over and, before retiring to our tents for the night, we walked over to the edge of the high *mesa* and, in the gathering shadows of twilight, looked down into the depths of that beautiful lake, knowing that probably we should never see it again.

And indeed, in all the years I spent in Arizona afterward, I never even heard of the lake again.

I wonder now, did it really exist or was it an illusion, a dream, or the mirage which appears to the desert traveller, to satisfy him and lure him on, to quiet his imagination, and to save his senses from utter extinction?

In the morning the camp was all astir for an early move. We had no time to look back: we were starting for a long day's march, across the "divide," and into Camp Verde.

But we soon found that the road (if road it could be called) was worse than any we had encountered. The ambulance was pitched and jerked from rock to rock and we were thumped against the iron framework in a most dangerous manner. So we got out and picked our way over the great sharp boulders.

The Alsatian soldier carried the baby, who lay securely in the *papoose* cradle.

One of the cavalry escort suggested my taking his horse, but I did not feel strong enough to think of mounting a horse, so great was my discouragement and so exhausted was my vitality. Oh! if girls only knew about these things I thought! For just a little knowledge of the care of an infant and its needs, its nourishment and its habits, might have saved both mother and child from such utter collapse.

Little by little we gave up hope of reaching Verde that day. At four o'clock we crossed the "divide," and clattered down a road so near the edge of a precipice that I was frightened beyond everything: my senses nearly left me. Down and around, this way and that, near the edge, then back again, swaying, swerving, pitching, the gravel clattering over the precipice, the six mules trotting their fastest, we reached the bottom and the driver pulled up his team. "Beaver Springs!" said he, impressively, loosening up the brakes.

As Jack lifted me out of the ambulance, I said: "Why didn't you tell me?" pointing back to the steep road.

"Oh," said he, "I thought it was better for you not to know; people get scared about such things, when they know about them before hand."

"But," I remarked, "such a break-neck pace!" Then, to the driver, "Smith, how could you drive down that place at such a rate and frighten me so?"

"Had to, ma'am, or we'd a'gone over the edge."

I had been brought up in a flat country down near the sea, and I did not know the dangers of mountain travelling, nor the difficulties attending the piloting of a six-mule team down a road like that. From this time on, however, Smith rose in my estimation. I seemed also to be realizing that the Southwest was a great country and that there was much to learn about. Life out there was beginning to interest me.

Camp Verde lay sixteen miles farther on; no one knew if the

road were good or bad. I declared I could not travel another mile, even if they all went on and left me to the wolves and the darkness of Beaver Springs.

We looked to our provisions and took account of stock. There was not enough for the two families. We had no flour and no bread; there was only a small piece of bacon, six potatoes, some condensed milk, and some chocolate. The Baileys decided to go on; for Mrs. Bailey was to meet her sister at Verde and her parents at Whipple. We said goodbye, and their ambulance rolled away. Our tent was pitched and the baby was laid on the bed, asleep from pure exhaustion.

The dread darkness of night descended upon us, and the strange odours of the bottom-lands arose, mingling with the delicious smoky smell of the camp-fire.

By the light of the blazing mesquite wood, we now divided what provisions we had, into two portions: one for supper, and one for breakfast. A very light meal we had that evening, and I arose from the mess-table unsatisfied and hungry.

Jack and I sat down by the camp-fire, musing over the hard times we were having, when suddenly I heard a terrified cry from my little son. We rushed to the tent, lighted a candle, and oh! horror upon horrors! his head and face were covered with large black ants; he was wailing helplessly, and beating the air with his tiny arms.

"My God!" cried Jack, "we're camped over an ant-hill!"

I seized the child, and brushing off the ants as I fled, brought him out to the fire, where by its light I succeeded in getting rid of them all. But the horror of it! Can any mother brought up in God's country with kind nurses and loved ones to minister to her child, for a moment imagine how I felt when I saw those hideous, three-bodied, long-legged black ants crawling over my baby's face? After a lapse of years, I cannot recall that moment without a shudder.

The soldiers at last found a place which seemed to be free from ant-hills, and our tent was again pitched, but only to find that the venomous things swarmed over us as soon as we lay down to rest.

And so, after the fashion of the Missouri emigrant, we climbed into the ambulance and lay down upon our blankets in the bottom of it, and tried to believe we were comfortable.

My long, hard journey of the preceding autumn, covering a period of two months; my trying experiences during the winter at Camp Apache; the sudden break-up and the packing; the lack of assistance from a nurse; the terrors of the journey; the sympathy for my child, who suffered from many ailments and principally from lack of nourishment, added to the profound fatigue I felt, had reduced my strength to a minimum. I wonder that I lived, but something sustained me, and when we reached Camp Verde the next day, and drew up before Lieutenant O'Connell's quarters, and saw Mrs. O'Connell's kind face beaming to welcome us, I felt that here was relief at last.

The tall Alsatian handed the *papoose* cradle to Mrs. O'Connell.

"Gracious goodness! what is this?" cried the bewildered woman; "surely it cannot be your baby! You haven't turned entirely Indian, have you, amongst those wild Apaches?"

I felt sorry I had not taken him out of the basket before we arrived. I did not realize the impression it would make at Camp Verde. After all, they did not know anything about our life at Apache, or our rough travels to get back from there. Here were lace-curtained windows, well-dressed women, smart uniforms, and, in fact, civilization, compared with what we had left.

The women of the post gathered around the broad *piazza*, to see the wonder. But when they saw the poor little wan face, the blue eyes which looked sadly out at them from this rude cradle, the linen bandages covering the back of the head, they did not laugh any more, but took him and ministered to him, as only kind women can minister to a sick baby.

There was not much rest, however, for we had to sort and rearrange our things, and dress ourselves properly. (Oh! the luxury of a room and a tub, after that journey!) Jack put on his best uniform, and there was no end of visiting, in spite of the heat, which was considerable even at that early date in May. The day there would have been pleasant enough but for my wretched condition.

The next morning we set out for Fort Whipple, making a long day's march, and arriving late in the evening. The wife of the Quartermaster, a total stranger to me, received us, and before we had time to exchange the usual social platitudes, she gave one look at the baby, and put an end to any such attempts. "You have a sick child; give him to me;" then I told her some things, and she said: "I wonder he is alive." Then she took him under her charge and declared we should not leave her house until he was well again. She understood all about nursing, and day by day, under her good care, and Doctor Henry Lippincott's skilful treatment, I saw my baby brought back to life again. Can I ever forget Mrs. Aldrich's blessed kindness?

Up to then, I had taken no interest in Camp MacDowell, where was stationed the company into which my husband was promoted. I knew it was somewhere in the southern part of the Territory, and isolated. The present was enough. I was meeting my old Fort Russell friends, and under Doctor Lippincott's good care I was getting back a measure of strength. Camp Mac-Dowell was not yet a reality to me.

We met again Colonel Wilkins and Mrs. Wilkins and Carrie, and Mrs. Wilkins thanked me for bringing her daughter alive out of those wilds. Poor girl; 'twas but a few months when we heard of her death, at the birth of her second child. I have always thought her death was caused by the long hard journey from Apache to Whipple, for Nature never intended women to go through what we went through, on that memorable journey by Stoneman's Lake.

There I met again Captain Porter, and I asked him if he had progressed any in his courtship, and he, being very much embarrassed, said he did not know, but if patient waiting was of any avail, he believed he might win his bride.

After we had been at Whipple a few days, Jack came in and remarked casually to Lieutenant Aldrich, "Well, I heard Bernard has asked to be relieved from Ehrenberg.

"What!" I said, "the lonely man down there on the river—the prisoner of Chillon—the silent one? Well, they are going to relieve him, of course?"

"Why, yes," said Jack, falteringly, "if they can get anyone to take his place."

"Can't they order some one?" I inquired.

"Of course they can," he replied, and then, turning towards the window, he ventured: "The fact is Martha, I've been offered it, and am thinking it over." (The real truth was, that he had applied for it, thinking it possessed great advantages over Camp MacDowell.)

"What! do I hear aright? Have your senses left you? Are you crazy? Are you going to take me to that awful place? Why, Jack, I should die there!"

"Now, Martha, be reasonable; listen to me, and if you really decide against it, I'll throw up the detail. But don't you see, we shall be right on the river, the boat comes up every fortnight or so, you can jump aboard and go up to San Francisco." (Oh, how alluring that sounded to my ears!) "Why, it's no trouble to get out of Arizona from Ehrenberg. Then, too, I shall be independent, and can do just as I like, and when I like," *et caetera, et caetera.* "Oh, you'll be making the greatest mistake, if you decide against it. As for MacDowell, it's a hell of a place, down there in the South; and you never will be able to go back East with the baby, if we once get settled down there. Why, it's a good fifteen days from the river."

And so he piled up the arguments in favour of Ehrenberg, saying finally, "You need not stop a day there. If the boat happens to be up, you can jump right aboard and start at once down river."

All the discomforts of the voyage on the *Newbern,* and the memory of those long days spent on the river steamer in August had paled before my recent experiences. I flew, in imagination, to the deck of the *Gila,* and to good Captain Mellon, who would take me and my child out of that wretched Territory.

"Yes, yes, let us go then," I cried; for here came in my inexperience. I thought I was choosing the lesser evil, and I knew that Jack believed it to be so, and also that he had set his heart upon Ehrenberg, for reasons known only to the understanding of a military man.

So it was decided to take the Ehrenberg detail.

CHAPTER 17

The Colorado Desert

Some serpents slid from out the grass
That grew in tufts by shattered stone,
Then hid below some broken mass
Of ruins older than the East,
That Time had eaten, as a bone
Is eaten by some savage beast.
Great dull-eyed rattlesnakes—they lay
All loathsome, yellow-skinned, and slept
Coiled tight as pine knots in the sun,
With flat heads through the centre run;
Then struck out sharp, then rattling crept
Flat-bellied down the dusty way.
                              —Joaquin Miller.

At the end of a week, we started forth for Ehrenberg. Our escort was now sent back to Camp Apache, and the Baileys remained at Fort Whipple, so our outfit consisted of one ambulance and one army wagon. One or two soldiers went along, to help with the teams and the camp.

We travelled two days over a semi-civilized country, and found quite comfortable ranches where we spent the nights. The greatest luxury was fresh milk, and we enjoyed that at these ranches in Skull Valley. They kept American cows, and supplied Whipple Barracks with milk and butter. We drank, and drank, and drank again, and carried a jugful to our bedside. The third day brought us to Cullen's ranch, at the edge of the desert. Mrs.

107

Cullen was a Mexican woman and had a little boy named Daniel; she cooked us a delicious supper of stewed chicken, and fried eggs, and good bread, and then she put our boy to bed in Daniel's crib. I felt so grateful to her; and with a return of physical comfort, I began to think that life, after all, might be worth the living.

Hopefully and cheerfully the next morning we entered the vast Colorado desert. This was verily the desert, more like the desert which our imagination pictures, than the one we had crossed in September from Mojave. It seemed so white, so bare, so endless, and so still; irreclaimable, eternal, like Death itself. The stillness was appalling. We saw great numbers of lizards darting about like lightning; they were nearly as white as the sand itself, and sat up on their hind legs and looked at us with their pretty, beady black eyes. It seemed very far off from everywhere and everybody, this desert—but I knew there was a camp somewhere awaiting us, and our mules trotted patiently on.

Towards noon they began to raise their heads and sniff the air; they knew that water was near. They quickened their pace, and we soon drew up before a large wooden structure. There were no trees nor grass around it. A Mexican worked the machinery with the aid of a mule, and water was bought for our twelve animals, at so much per head.

The place was called Mesquite Wells; the man dwelt alone in his desolation, with no living being except his mule for company. How could he endure it! I was not able, even faintly, to comprehend it; I had not lived long enough. He occupied a small hut, and there he staid, year in and year out, selling water to the passing traveller; and I fancy that travellers were not so frequent at Mesquite Wells a quarter of a century ago.

The thought of that hermit and his dreary surroundings filled my mind for a long time after we drove away, and it was only when we halted and a soldier got down to kill a great rattlesnake near the ambulance, that my thoughts were diverted. The man brought the rattles to us and the new toy served to amuse my little son.

At night we arrived at Desert Station. There was a good ranch there, kept by Hunt and Dudley, Englishmen, I believe. I did not see them, but I wondered who they were and why they staid in such a place. They were absent at the time; perhaps they had mines or something of the sort to look after. One is always imagining things about people who live in such extraordinary places.

At all events, whatever Messrs. Hunt and Dudley were doing down there, their ranch was clean and attractive, which was more than could be said of the place where we stopped the next night, a place called Tyson's Wells. We slept in our tent that night, for of all places on the earth a poorly kept ranch in Arizona is the most melancholy and uninviting. It reeks of everything unclean, morally and physically. Owen Wister has described such a place in his delightful story, where the young tenderfoot dances for the amusement of the old *habitués*.

One more day's travel across the desert brought us to our El Dorado.

CHAPTER 18

Ehrenberg on the Colorado

Under the burning midday sun of Arizona, on May 16th, our six good mules, with the long whip cracking about their ears, and the ambulance rattling merrily along, brought us into the village of Ehrenberg. There was one street, so called, which ran along on the river bank, and then a few cross streets straggling back into the desert, with here and there a low *adobe casa*. The Government house stood not far from the river, and as we drove up to the entrance the same blank white walls stared at me. It did not look so much like a prison, after all, I thought.

Captain Bernard, the man whom I had pitied, stood at the doorway, to greet us, and after we were inside the house he had some biscuits and wine brought; and then the change of stations was talked of, and he said to me, "Now, please make yourself at home. The house is yours; my things are virtually packed up, and I leave in a day or two. There is a soldier here who can stay with you; he has been able to attend to my simple wants. I eat only twice a day; and here is Charley, my Indian, who fetches the water from the river and does the chores. I dine generally at sundown."

A shadow fell across the sunlight in the doorway; I looked around and there stood "Charley," who had come in with the noiseless step of the *moccasined* foot. I saw before me a handsome naked Cocopah Indian, who wore a belt and a gee-string. He seemed to feel at home and began to help with the bags and various paraphernalia of ambulance travellers. He looked to be about twenty-four years old. His face was smiling and friendly and I knew I should like him.

The house was a one-story *adobe*. It formed two sides of a hollow square; the other two sides were a high wall, and the Government freight-house respectively. The courtyard was partly shaded by a *ramada* and partly open to the hot sun. There was a chicken-yard in one corner of the inclosed square, and in the centre stood a rickety old pump, which indicated some sort of a well. Not a green leaf or tree or blade of grass in sight. Nothing but white sand, as far as one could see, in all directions.

Inside the house there were bare white walls, ceilings covered with manta, and sagging, as they always do; small windows set in deep embrasures, and *adobe* floors. Small and inconvenient rooms, opening one into another around two sides of the square. A sort of low veranda protected by lattice screens, made from a species of slim cactus, called *ocotilla*, woven together, and bound with rawhide, ran around a part of the house.

Our dinner was enlivened by some good Cocomonga wine. I tried to ascertain something about the source of provisions, but evidently the soldier had done the foraging, and Captain Bernard admitted that it was difficult, adding always that he did not require much, "it was so warm," *et caetera, et caetera*. The next morning I took the reins, nominally, but told the soldier to go ahead and do just as he had always done. I selected a small room for the baby's bath, the all important function of the day.

The Indian brought me a large tub (the same sort of a half of a vinegar barrel we had used at Apache for ourselves), set it down in the middle of the floor, and brought water from a barrel which stood in the corral. A low box was placed for me to sit on. This was a bachelor establishment, and there was no place but the floor to lay things on; but what with the splashing and the leaking and the dripping, the floor turned to mud and the white clothes and towels were covered with it, and I myself was a sight to behold. The Indian stood smiling at my plight. He spoke only a pigeon English, but said, "too much-ee wet."

I was in despair; things began to look hopeless again to me.

111

I thought "surely these Mexicans must know how to manage with these floors." Fisher, the steamboat agent, came in, and I asked him if he could not find me a nurse. He said he would try, and went out to see what could be done.

He finally brought in a rather forlorn looking Mexican woman leading a little child (whose father was not known), and she said she would come to us for *quinze pesos* a month. I consulted with Fisher, and he said she was a pretty good sort, and that we could not afford to be too particular down in that country. And so she came; and although she was indolent, and forever smoking cigarettes, she did care for the baby, and fanned him when he slept, and proved a blessing to me.

And now came the unpacking of our boxes, which had floated down the Colorado Chiquito. The fine damask, brought from Germany for my linen chest, was a mass of mildew; and when the books came to light, I could have wept to see the pretty editions of Schiller, Goethe, and Lessing, which I had bought in Hanover, fall out of their bindings; the latter, warped out of all shape, and some of them unrecognizable. I did the best I could, however, not to show too much concern, and gathered the pages carefully together, to dry them in the sun.

They were my pride, my best beloved possessions, the links that bound me to the happy days in old Hanover.

I went to Fisher for everything—a large, well-built American, and a kind good man. Mrs. Fisher could not endure the life at Ehrenberg, so she lived in San Francisco, he told me. There were several other white men in the place, and two large stores where everything was kept that people in such countries buy. These merchants made enormous profits, and their families lived in luxury in San Francisco.

The rest of the population consisted of a very poor class of Mexicans, Cocopah, Yuma and Mojave Indians, and half-breeds.

The duties of the army officer stationed here consisted principally in receiving and shipping the enormous quantity of Government freight which was landed by the river steamers. It was shipped by wagon trains across the Territory, and at all times the work carried large responsibilities with it.

I soon realized that however much the present incumbent might like the situation, it was no fit place for a woman.

The station at Ehrenberg was what we call, in the army, "detached service." I realized that we had left the army for the time being; that we had cut loose from a garrison; that we were in a place where good food could not be procured, and where there were practically no servants to be had. That there was not a woman to speak to, or to go to for advice or help, and, worst of all, that there was no doctor in the place. Besides all this, my clothes were all ruined by lying wet for a fortnight in the boxes, and I had practically nothing to wear. I did not then know what useless things clothes were in Ehrenberg.

The situation appeared rather serious; the weather had grown intensely hot, and it was decided that the only thing for me to do was to go to San Francisco for the summer.

So one day we heard the whistle of the *Gila* going up; and when she came down river, I was all ready to go on board, with Patrocina and Jesusita,[1] and my own child, who was yet but five months old. I bade farewell to the man on detached service, and we headed down river. We seemed to go down very rapidly, although the trip lasted several days. Patrocina took to her bed with neuralgia (or nostalgia); her little devil of a child screamed the entire days and nights through, to the utter discomfiture of the few other passengers. A young lieutenant and his wife and an army surgeon, who had come from one of the posts in the interior, were among the number, and they seemed to think that I could help it (though they did not say so).

Finally the doctor said that if I did not throw Jesusita overboard, he would; why didn't I "wring the neck of its worthless Mexican of a mother?" and so on, until I really grew very nervous and unhappy, thinking what I should do after we got on board the ocean steamer. I, a victim of seasickness, with this unlucky woman and her child on my hands, in addition to my

---

1. Diminutive of Jesus, a very common name amongst the Mexicans. Pronounced Hay-soo-se-ta.

own! No; I made up my mind to go back to Ehrenberg, but I said nothing.

I did not dare to let Doctor Clark know of my decision, for I knew he would try to dissuade me; but when we reached the mouth of the river, and they began to transfer the passengers to the ocean steamer which lay in the offing, I quietly sat down upon my trunk and told them I was going back to Ehrenberg. Captain Mellon grinned; the others were speechless; they tried persuasion, but saw it was useless; and then they said goodbye to me, and our stern-wheeler headed about and started for up river.

Ehrenberg had become truly my old man of the sea; I could not get rid of it. There I must go, and there I must stay, until circumstances and the Fates were more propitious for my departure.

CHAPTER 19

Summer at Ehrenberg

The week we spent going up the Colorado in June was not as uncomfortable as the time spent on the river in August of the previous year. Everything is relative, I discovered, and I was happy in going back to stay with the First Lieutenant of C Company, and share his fortunes awhile longer.

Patrocina recovered, as soon as she found we were to return to Ehrenberg. I wondered how anybody could be so homesick for such a God-forsaken place. I asked her if she had ever seen a tree, or green grass (for I could talk with her quite easily now). She shook her mournful head. "But don't you want to see trees and grass and flowers?"

Another sad shake of the head was the only reply.

Such people, such natures, and such lives, were incomprehensible to me then. I could not look at things except from my own standpoint.

She took her child upon her knee, and lighted a cigarette; I took mine upon my knee, and gazed at the river banks: they were now old friends: I had gazed at them many times before; how much I had experienced, and how much had happened since I first saw them! Could it be that I should ever come to love them, and the pungent smell of the arrow-weed which covered them to the water's edge?

The huge mosquitoes swarmed over us in the nights from those thick clumps of arrow-weed and willow, and the nets with which Captain Mellon provided us did not afford much protection.

The June heat was bad enough, though not quite so stifling as the August heat. I was becoming accustomed to climates, and had learned to endure discomfort. The salt beef and the Chinaman's peach pies were no longer offensive to me. Indeed, I had a good appetite for them, though they were not exactly the sort of food prescribed by the modern doctor, for a young mother. Of course, milk, eggs, and all fresh food were not to be had on the river boats. Ice was still a thing unknown on the Colorado.

When, after a week, the *Gila* pushed her nose up to the bank at Ehrenberg, there stood the quartermaster. He jumped aboard, and did not seem in the least surprised to see me. "I knew you'd come back," said he. I laughed, of course, and we both laughed.

"I hadn't the courage to go on," I replied

"Oh, well, we can make things comfortable here and get through the summer some way," he said. "I'll build some rooms on, and a kitchen, and we can surely get along. It's the healthiest place in the world for children, they tell me."

So after a hearty handshake with Captain Mellon, who had taken such good care of me on my week's voyage up river, I being almost the only passenger, I put my foot once more on the shores of old Ehrenberg, and we wended our way towards the blank white walls of the Government house. I was glad to be back, and content to wait.

So work was begun immediately on the kitchen. My first stipulation was, that the new rooms were to have wooden floors; for, although the Cocopah Charley kept the *adobe* floors in perfect condition, by sprinkling them down and sweeping them out every morning, they were quite impossible, especially where it concerned white dresses and children, and the little sharp rocks in them seemed to be so tiring to the feet.

Life as we Americans live it was difficult in Ehrenberg. I often said: "Oh! if we could only live as the Mexicans live, how easy it would be!" For they had their fire built between some stones piled up in their yard, a piece of sheet iron laid over the top: this was the cooking-stove. A pot of coffee was made in the morning early, and the family sat on the low porch and drank it, and ate a biscuit. Then a kettle of *frijoles* [2] was put over to boil. These were boiled slowly for some hours, then lard and salt were added, and they simmered down until they were deliciously fit to eat, and had a thick red gravy.

Then the young matron, or daughter of the house, would mix the peculiar paste of flour and salt and water, for *tortillas*, a species of unleavened bread. These *tortillas* were patted out until they were as large as a dinner plate, and very thin; then thrown onto the hot sheet-iron, where they baked. Each one of the family then got a *tortilla*, the spoonful of beans was laid upon it, and so they managed without the paraphernalia of silver and china and napery.

How I envied them the simplicity of their lives! Besides, the *tortillas* were delicious to eat, and as for the frijoles, they were beyond anything I had ever eaten in the shape of beans. I took lessons in the making of *tortillas*. A woman was paid to come and teach me; but I never mastered the art. It is in the blood of the Mexican, and a girl begins at a very early age to make the *tortilla*. It is the most graceful thing to see a pretty Mexican toss the wafer-like disc over her bare arm, and pat it out until transparent.

This was their supper; for, like nearly all people in the tropics, they ate only twice a day. Their fare was varied sometimes by a little *carni seca*, pounded up and stewed with *chile verde* or *chile colorado*.

Now if you could hear the soft, exquisite, affectionate drawl with which the Mexican woman says *chile verde* you could perhaps come to realize what an important part the delicious green pepper plays in the cookery of these countries. They do not use it in its raw state, but generally roast it whole, stripping off the thin skin and throwing away the seeds, leaving only the pulp, which acquires a fine flavour by having been roasted or toasted over the hot coals.

The women were scrupulously clean and modest, and always

---

2. Mexican brown bean.

wore, when in their *casa*, a low-necked and short-sleeved white linen *camisa*, fitting neatly, with bands around neck and arms. Over this they wore a calico skirt; always white stockings and black slippers. When they ventured out, the younger women put on muslin gowns, and carried parasols. The older women wore a linen towel thrown over their heads, or, in cool weather, the black *riboso*. I often cried: "Oh! if I could only dress as the Mexicans do! Their necks and arms do look so cool and clean."

I have always been sorry I did not adopt their fashion of house apparel. Instead of that, I yielded to the prejudices of my conservative partner, and sweltered during the day in high-necked and long-sleeved white dresses, kept up the table in American fashion, ate American food in so far as we could get it, and all at the expense of strength; for our soldier cooks, who were loaned us by Captain Ernest from his company at Fort Yuma, were constantly being changed, and I was often left with the Indian and the indolent Patrocina. At those times, how I wished I had no silver, no table linen, no china, and could revert to the primitive customs of my neighbours!

There was no market, but occasionally a Mexican killed a steer, and we bought enough for one meal; but having no ice, and no place away from the terrific heat, the meat was hung out under the *ramada* with a piece of netting over it, until the first heat had passed out of it, and then it was cooked.

The Mexican, after selling what meat he could, cut the rest into thin strips and hung it up on ropes to dry in the sun. It dried hard and brittle, in its natural state, so pure is the air on that wonderful river bank. They called this *carni seca*, and the Americans called it "jerked beef."

Patrocina often prepared me a dish of this, when I was unable to taste the fresh meat. She would pound it fine with a heavy pestle, and then put it to simmer, seasoning it with the green or red pepper. It was most savoury. There was no butter at all during the hot months, but our hens laid a few eggs, and the quartermaster was allowed to keep a small lot of commissary stores, from which we drew our supplies of flour, ham, and canned things. We were often without milk for weeks at a time, for the cows crossed the river to graze, and sometimes could not get back until the river fell again, and they could pick their way back across the shifting sand bars.

The Indian brought the water every morning in buckets from the river. It looked like melted chocolate. He filled the barrels, and when it had settled clear, the *ollas* were filled, and thus the drinking water was a trifle cooler than the air. One day it seemed unusually cool, so I said: "Let us see by the thermometer how cool the water really is." We found the temperature of the water to be 86 degrees; but that, with the air at 122 in the shade, seemed quite refreshing to drink.

I did not see any white people at all except Fisher, Abe Frank (the mail contractor), and one or two of the younger merchants. If I wanted anything, I went to Fisher. He always could solve the difficulty. He procured for me an excellent middle-aged laundress, who came and brought the linen herself, and, bowing to the floor, said always, "*Buenos dias, Senorita!*" dwelling on the latter word, as a gentle compliment to a younger woman, and then, "*Mucho calor este dia,*" in her low, drawling voice.

Like the others, she was spotlessly clean, modest and gentle. I asked her what on earth they did about bathing, for I had found the tub baths with the muddy water so disagreeable. She told me the women bathed in the river at daybreak, and asked me if I would like to go with them.

I was only too glad to avail myself of her invitation, and so, like Pharoah's daughter of old, I went with my gentle handmaiden every morning to the river bank, and, wading in about knee-deep in the thick red waters, we sat down and let the swift current flow by us. We dared not go deeper; we could feel the round stones grinding against each other as they were carried down, and we were all afraid. It was difficult to keep one's foothold, and Captain Mellon's words were ever ringing in my ears, "He who disappears below the surface of the Colorado is never seen again." But we joined hands and ventured like children and played like children in these red waters and after all, it was much nicer than a tub of muddy water indoors.

A clump of low mesquite trees at the top of the bank afforded sufficient protection at that hour; we rubbed dry, slipped on a loose gown, and wended our way home. What a contrast to the limpid, bracing salt waters of my own beloved shores!

When I thought of them, I was seized with a longing which consumed me and made my heart sick; and I thought of these poor people, who had never known anything in their lives but those desert places, and that muddy red water, and wondered what they would do, how they would act, if transported into some beautiful forest, or to the cool bright shores where clear blue waters invite to a plunge.

Whenever the river-boat came up, we were sure to have guests, for many officers went into the Territory *via* Ehrenberg. Sometimes the "transportation" was awaiting them; at other times, they were obliged to wait at Ehrenberg until it arrived. They usually lived on the boat, as we had no extra rooms, but I generally asked them to luncheon or supper (for anything that could be called a dinner was out of the question).

This caused me some anxiety, as there was nothing to be had; but I remembered the hospitality I had received, and thought of what they had been obliged to eat on the voyage, and I always asked them to share what we could provide, however simple it might be.

At such times we heard all the news from Washington and the States, and all about the fashions, and they, in their turn, asked me all sorts of questions about Ehrenberg and how I managed to endure the life. They were always astonished when the *Cocopah* Indian waited on them at table, for he wore nothing but his gee-string, and although it was an everyday matter to us, it rather took their breath away.

But "Charley" appealed to my aesthetic sense in every way. Tall, and well-made, with clean-cut limbs and features, fine smooth copper-coloured skin, handsome face, heavy black hair done up in *pompadour* fashion and plastered with Colorado mud, which was baked white by the sun, a small feather at the crown of his head, wide turquoise bead bracelets upon his upper arm, and a knife at his waist—this was my Charley, my half-tame Cocopah, my man about the place, my butler in fact, for Charley understood how to open a bottle of Cocomonga gracefully, and to keep the glasses filled.

Charley also wheeled the baby out along the river banks, for we had had a fine "perambulator" sent down from San Francisco. It was an incongruous sight, to be sure, and one must laugh to think of it. The Ehrenberg babies did not have carriages, and the village flocked to see it. There sat the fair-haired, six-months-old boy, with but one linen garment on, no cap, no stockings—and this wild man of the desert, his knife gleaming at his waist, and his gee-string floating out behind, wheeling and pushing the carriage along the sandy roads.

But this came to an end; for one day Fisher rushed in, breathless, and said: "Well! here is your baby! I was just in time, for that Injun of yours left the carriage in the middle of the street, to look in at the store window, and a herd of wild cattle came tearing down! I grabbed the carriage to the sidewalk, cussed the Injun out, and here's the child! It's no use," he added, "you can't trust those Injuns out of sight."

The heat was terrific. Our cots were placed in the open part of the corral (as our courtyard was always called). It was a desolate-looking place; on one side, the high *adobe* wall; on another, the freight-house; and on the other two, our apartments. Our kitchen and the two other rooms were now completed. The kitchen had no windows, only open spaces to admit the air and light, and we were often startled in the night by the noise of thieves in the house, rummaging for food.

At such times, our soldier-cook would rush into the corral with his rifle, the lieutenant would jump up and seize his shotgun, which always stood nearby, and together they would roam through the house. But the thieving Indians could jump out of the windows as easily as they jumped in, and the excitement would soon be over. The violent sand-storms which prevail in those deserts, sometimes came up in the night, without warning;

then we rushed half suffocated and blinded into the house, and as soon as we had closed the windows it had passed on, leaving a deep layer of sand on everything in the room, and on our perspiring bodies.

Then came the work, next day, for the Indian had to carry everything out of doors; and one storm was so bad that he had to use a shovel to remove the sand from the floors. The desert literally blew into the house.

And now we saw a singular phenomenon. In the late afternoon of each day, a hot steam would collect over the face of the river, then slowly rise, and floating over the length and breadth of this wretched hamlet of Ehrenberg, descend upon and envelop us. Thus we wilted and perspired, and had one part of the vapour bath without its bracing concomitant of the cool shower. In a half hour it was gone, but always left me prostrate; then Jack gave me milk punch, if milk was at hand, or sherry and egg, or something to bring me up to normal again. We got to dread the steam so; it was the climax of the long hot day and was peculiar to that part of the river.

The paraphernalia by the side of our cots at night consisted of a pitcher of cold tea, a lantern, matches, a revolver, and a shotgun. Enormous yellow cats, which lived in and around the freight-house, darted to and fro inside and outside the house, along the ceiling-beams, emitting loud cries, and that alone was enough to prevent sleep. In the old part of the house, some of the partitions did not run up to the roof, but were left open (for ventilation, I suppose), thus making a fine play-ground for cats and rats, which darted along, squeaking, meowing and clattering all the night through.

An uncanny feeling of insecurity was ever with me. What with the accumulated effect of the day's heat, what with the thieving Indians, the sand-storms and the cats, our nights by no means gave us the refreshment needed by our worn-out systems. By the latter part of the summer, I was so exhausted by the heat and the various difficulties of living, that I had become a mere shadow of my former self.

Men and children seem to thrive in those climates, but it is death to women, as I had often heard.

It was in the late summer that the boat arrived one day bringing a large number of staff officers and their wives, head clerks, and "general service" men for Fort Whipple. They had all been stationed in Washington for a number of years, having had what is known in the army as "gilt-edged" details. I threw a linen towel over my head, and went to the boat to call on them, and, remembering my voyage from San Francisco the year before, prepared to sympathize with them. But they had met their fate with resignation; knowing they should find a good climate and a pleasant post up in the mountains, and as they had no young children with them, they were disposed to make merry over their discomforts.

We asked them to come to our quarters for supper, and to come early, as any place was cooler than the boat, lying down there in the melting sun, and nothing to look upon but those hot zinc-covered decks or the ragged river banks, with their uninviting huts scattered along the edge.

The surroundings somehow did not fit these people. Now Mrs. Montgomery at Camp Apache seemed to have adapted herself to the rude setting of a log cabin in the mountains, but these were Staff people and they had enjoyed for years the civilized side of army life; now they were determined to rough it, but they did not know how to begin.

The beautiful wife of the adjutant-general was mourning over some freckles which had come to adorn her dazzling complexion, and she had put on a large hat with a veil. Was there ever anything so incongruous as a hat and veil in Ehrenberg! For a long time I had not seen a woman in a hat; the Mexicans all wore a linen towel over their heads.

But her beauty was startling, and, after all, I thought, a woman so handsome must try to live up to her reputation. Now for some weeks Jack had been investigating the sulphur well, which was beneath the old pump in our corral. He had had a long wooden bath-tub built, and I watched it with a lazy interest, and observed his glee as he found a longshoreman or roustabout who could caulk it. The shape was exactly like a coffin (but men have no imaginations), and when I told him how it made me feel to look at it, he said: "Oh! you are always thinking of gloomy things. It's a fine tub, and we are mighty lucky to find that man to caulk it. I'm going to set it up in the little square room, and lead the sulphur water into it, and it will be splendid, and just think," he added, "what it will do for rheumatism!"

Now Jack had served in the Twentieth Massachusetts Volunteers during the Civil War, and the swamps of the Chickahominy had brought him into close acquaintance with that dread disease.

As for myself, rheumatism was about the only ailment I did not have at that time, and I suppose I did not really sympathize with him. But this energetic and indomitable man mended the pump, with Fisher's help, and led the water into the house, laid a floor, set up the tub in the little square room, and behold, our sulphur bath!

After much persuasion, I tried the bath. The water flowed thick and inky black into the tub; of course the odour was beyond description, and the effect upon me was not such that I was ever willing to try it again. Jack beamed. "How do you like it, Martha?" said he. "Isn't it fine? Why people travel hundreds of miles to get a bath like that!"

I had my own opinion, but I did not wish to dampen his enthusiasm. Still, in order to protect myself in the future, I had to tell him I thought I should ordinarily prefer the river.

"Well," he said, "there are those who will be thankful to have a bath in that water; I am going to use it every day."

I remonstrated: "How do you know what is in that inky water—and how do you dare to use it?"

"Oh, Fisher says it's all right; people here used to drink it years ago, but they have not done so lately, because the pump was broken down."

The Washington people seemed glad to pay us the visit. Jack's eyes danced with true generosity and glee. He marked his victim; and, selecting the Staff beauty and the Paymaster's wife, he expatiated on the wonderful properties of his sulphur bath.

"Why, yes, the sooner the better," said Mrs. Martin. "I'd give everything I have in this world, and all my chances for the next, to get a tub bath!"

"It will be so refreshing just before supper," said Mrs. Maynadier, who was more conservative.

So the Indian, who had put on his dark blue waist-band (or sash), made from flannel, revelled out and twisted into strands of yarn, and which showed the supple muscles of his clean-cut thighs, and who had done up an extra high pompadour in white clay, and burnished his knife, which gleamed at his waist, ushered these Washington women into a small apartment adjoining the bath-room, and turned on the inky stream into the sarcophagus.

The Staff beauty looked at the black pool, and shuddered. "Do you use it?" said she.

"Occasionally," I equivocated.

"Does it hurt the complexion?" she ventured.

"Jack thinks it excellent for that," I replied.

And then I left them, directing Charley to wait, and prepare the bath for the second victim.

By and by the beauty came out. "Where is your mirror?" cried she (for our appointments were primitive, and mirrors did not grow on bushes at Ehrenberg); "I fancy I look queer," she added, and, in truth, she did; for our water of the Styx did not seem to affiliate with the chemical properties of the numerous cosmetics used by her, more or less, all her life, but especially on the voyage, and her face had taken on a queer colour, with peculiar spots here and there.

Fortunately my mirrors were neither large nor true, and she never really saw how she looked, but when she came back into the living-room, she laughed and said to Jack: "What kind of water did you say that was? I never saw any just like it."

"Oh! you have probably never been much to the sulphur springs," said he, with his most superior and crushing manner.

"Perhaps not," she replied, "but I thought I knew something about it; why, my entire body turned such a queer colour."

"Oh! it always does that," said this optimistic soldier man, "and that shows it is doing good."

The paymaster's wife joined us later. I think she had profited by the beauty's experience, for she said but little.

The quartermaster was happy; and what if his wife did not believe in that uncanny stream which flowed somewhere from out the infernal regions, underlying that wretched hamlet, he had succeeded in being a benefactor to two travellers at least!

We had a merry supper: cold ham, chicken, and fresh biscuit, a plenty of good Cocomonga wine, sweet milk, which to be sure turned to curds as it stood on the table, some sort of preserves from a tin, and good coffee. I gave them the best to be had in the desert—and at all events it was a change from the Chinaman's salt beef and peach pies, and they saw fresh table linen and shining silver, and accepted our simple hospitality in the spirit in which we gave it.

Alice Martin was much amused over Charley; and Charley could do nothing but gaze on her lovely features. "Why on earth don't you put some clothes on him?" laughed she, in her delightful way.

I explained to her that the Indian's fashion of wearing white men's clothes was not pleasing to the eye, and told her that she must cultivate her aesthetic sense, and in a short time she would be able to admire these copper-coloured creatures of Nature as much as I did.

But I fear that a life spent mostly in a large city had cast fetters around her imagination, and that the life at Fort Whipple afterwards savoured too much of civilization to loosen the bonds of her soul. I saw her many times again, but she never recovered from her amazement at Charley's lack of apparel, and she never forgot the sulphur bath.

CHAPTER 20

My Deliverer

One day, in the early autumn, as the *Gila* touched at Ehren-berg, on her way down river, Captain Mellon called Jack on to the boat, and, pointing to a young woman, who was about to go ashore, said: "Now, there's a girl I think will do for your wife. She imagines she has bronchial troubles, and some doctor has ordered her to Tucson. She comes from up North somewhere. Her money has given out, and she thinks I am going to leave her here. Of course, you know I would not do that; I can take her on down to Yuma, but I thought your wife might like to have her, so I've told her she could not travel on this boat any farther without she could pay her fare. Speak to her: she looks to me like a nice sort of a girl."

In the meantime, the young woman had gone ashore and was sitting upon her trunk, gazing hopelessly about. Jack approached, offered her a home and good wages, and brought her to me.

I could have hugged her for very joy, but I restrained myself and advised her to stay with us for awhile, saying the Ehrenberg climate was quite as good as that of Tucson.

She remarked quietly: "You do not look as if it agreed with you very well, ma'am."

Then I told her of my young child, and my hard journeys, and she decided to stay until she could earn enough to reach Tucson.

And so Ellen became a member of our Ehrenberg family. She was a fine, strong girl, and a very good cook, and seemed to be in perfect health. She said, however, that she had had an obstinate cough which nothing would reach, and that was why she came to Arizona. From that time, things went more smoothly. Some yeast was procured from the Mexican bakeshop, and Ellen baked bread and other things, which seemed like the greatest luxuries to us. We sent the soldier back to his company at Fort Yuma, and began to live with a degree of comfort.

I looked at Ellen as my deliverer, and regarded her coming as a special providence, the kind I had heard about all my life in New England, but had never much believed in.

After a few weeks, Ellen was one evening seized with a dreadful toothache, which grew so severe that she declared she could not endure it another hour: she must have the tooth out. "Was there a dentist in the place?"

I looked at Jack: he looked at me: Ellen groaned with pain.

"Why, yes! of course there is," said this man for emergencies; "Fisher takes out teeth, he told me so the other day."

Now I did not believe that Fisher knew any more about extracting teeth than I did myself, but I breathed a prayer to the Recording Angel, and said naught.

"I'll go get Fisher," said Jack.

Now Fisher was the steamboat agent. He stood six feet in his stockings, had a powerful physique and a determined eye. Men in those countries had to be determined; for if they once lost their nerve, Heaven save them. Fisher had handsome black eyes.

When they came in, I said: "Can you attend to this business, Mr. Fisher?"

"I think so," he replied, quietly. "The Quartermaster says he has some forceps."

I gasped. Jack, who had left the room, now appeared, a box of instruments in his hand, his eyes shining with joy and triumph.

Fisher took the box, and scanned it. "I guess they'll do," said he.

So we placed Ellen in a chair, a stiff barrack chair, with a rawhide seat, and no arms.

It was evening.

"Mattie, you must hold the candle," said Jack. "I'll hold Ellen, and, Fisher, you pull the tooth."

So I lighted the candle, and held it, while Ellen tried, by its flickering light, to show Fisher the tooth that ached.

Fisher looked again at the box of instruments. "Why," said he, "these are lower jaw rollers, the kind used a hundred years ago; and her tooth is an upper jaw."

"Never mind," answered the lieutenant, "the instruments are all right. Fisher, you can get the tooth out, that's all you want, isn't it?"

The lieutenant was impatient; and besides he did not wish any slur cast upon his precious instruments.

So Fisher took up the forceps, and clattered around amongst Ellen's sound white teeth. His hand shook, great beads of perspiration gathered on his face, and I perceived a very strong odour of Cocomonga wine. He had evidently braced for the occasion.

It was, however, too late to protest. He fastened onto a molar, and with the lion's strength which lay in his gigantic frame, he wrenched it out.

Ellen put up her hand and felt the place. "My God! you've pulled the wrong tooth!" cried she, and so he had.

I seized a jug of red wine which stood nearby, and poured out a gobletful, which she drank. The blood came freely from her mouth, and I feared something dreadful had happened.

Fisher declared she had shown him the wrong tooth, and was perfectly willing to try again. I could not witness the second attempt, so I put the candle down and fled.

The stout-hearted and confiding girl allowed the second trial, and between the steamboat agent, the Lieutenant, and the red wine, the aching molar was finally extracted.

This was a serious and painful occurrence. It did not cause any of us to laugh, at the time. I am sure that Ellen, at least, never saw the comical side of it.

When it was all over, I thanked Fisher, and Jack beamed upon me with: "You see, Mattie, my case of instruments did come in handy, after all."

Encouraged by success, he applied for a pannier of medicines, and the Ehrenberg citizens soon regarded him as a healer. At a certain hour in the morning, the sick ones came to his office, and he dispensed simple drugs to them and was enabled to do much good. He seemed to have a sort of intuitive knowledge about medicines and performed some miraculous cures, but acquired little or no facility in the use of the language.

I was often called in as interpreter, and with the help of the sign language, and the little I knew of Spanish, we managed to get an idea of the ailments of these poor people.

And so our life flowed on in that desolate spot, by the banks of the Great Colorado.

I rarely went outside the enclosure, except for my bath in the river at daylight, or for some urgent matter. The one street along the river was hot and sandy and neglected. One had not only to wade through the sand, but to step over the dried heads or horns or bones of animals left there to whiten where they died, or thrown out, possibly, when someone killed a sheep or beef. Nothing decayed there, but dried and baked hard in that wonderful air and sun.

Then, the groups of Indians, squaws and half-breeds loafing around the village and the store! One never felt sure what one was to meet, and although by this time I tolerated about everything that I had been taught to think wicked or immoral, still, in Ehrenberg, the limit was reached, in the sights I saw on the village streets, too bold and too rude to be described in these pages.

The few white men there led respectable lives enough for that country. The standard was not high, and when I thought of the dreary years they had already spent there without their families, and the years they must look forward to remaining there, I was willing to reserve my judgement.

CHAPTER 21

Winter in Ehrenberg

We asked my sister, Mrs. Penniman, to come out and spend the winter with us, and to bring her son, who was in most delicate health. It was said that the climate of Ehrenberg would have a magical effect upon all diseases of the lungs or throat. So, to save her boy, my sister made the long and arduous trip out from New England, arriving in Ehrenberg in October.

What a joy to see her, and to initiate her into the ways of our life in Arizona! Everything was new, everything was a wonder to her and to my nephew. At first, he seemed to gain perceptibly, and we had great hopes of his recovery.

It was now cool enough to sleep indoors, and we began to know what it was to have a good night's rest.

But no sooner had we gotten one part of our life comfortably arranged, before another part seemed to fall out of adjustment. Accidents and climatic conditions kept my mind in a perpetual state of unrest.

Our dining-room door opened through two small rooms into the kitchen, and one day, as I sat at the table, waiting for Jack to come in to supper, I heard a strange sort of crashing noise. Looking towards the kitchen, through the vista of open doorways, I saw Ellen rush to the door which led to the courtyard. She turned a livid white, threw up her hands, and cried, "Great God! the Captain!" She was transfixed with horror.

I flew to the door, and saw that the pump had collapsed and gone down into the deep sulphur well. In a second, Jack's head and hands appeared at the edge; he seemed to be caught in the debris of rotten timber. Before I could get to him, he had scrambled half way out. "Don't come near this place," he cried, "it's all caving in!"

And so it seemed; for, as he worked himself up and out, the entire structure feel in, and half the corral with it, as it looked to me.

Jack escaped what might have been an unlucky bath in his sulphur well, and we all recovered our composure as best we could.

Surely, if life was dull at Ehrenberg, it could not be called exactly monotonous. We were not obliged to seek our excitement outside; we had plenty of it, such as it was, within our walls.

My confidence in Ehrenberg, however, as a salubrious dwelling-place, was being gradually and literally undermined. I began to be distrustful of the very ground beneath my feet. Ellen felt the same way, evidently, although we did not talk much about it. She probably longed also for some of her own kind; and when, one morning, we went into the dining-room for breakfast, Ellen stood, hat on, bag in hand, at the door. Dreading to meet my chagrin, she said: "Goodbye, Captain; goodbye, missis, you've been very kind to me. I'm leaving on the stage for Tucson—where I first started for, you know."

And she tripped out and climbed up into the dusty, rickety vehicle called "the stage." I had felt so safe about Ellen, as I did not know that any stage line ran through the place.

And now I was in a fine plight! I took a sunshade, and ran over to Fisher's house. "Mr. Fisher, what shall I do? Ellen has gone to Tucson!"

Fisher bethought himself, and we went out together in the village. Not a woman to be found who would come to cook for us! There was only one thing to do. The quartermaster was allowed a soldier, to assist in the Government work. I asked him if he understood cooking; he said he had never done any, but he would try, if I would show him how.

This proved a hopeless task, and I finally gave it up. Jack dispatched an Indian runner to Fort Yuma, ninety miles or more down river, begging Captain Ernest to send us a soldier-cook on the next boat.

This was a long time to wait; the inconveniences were intolerable: there were our four selves, Patrocina and Jesusita, the soldier-clerk and the Indian, to be provided for: Patrocina prepared *carni seca* with peppers, a little boy came around with *cuajada*, a delicious sweet curd cheese, and I tried my hand at bread, following out Ellen's instructions.

How often I said to my husband. "If we must live in this wretched place, let's give up civilization and live as the Mexicans do! They are the only happy beings around here.

"Look at them, as you pass along the street! At nearly any hour in the day you can see them, sitting under their *ramada*, their backs propped against the wall of their *casa*, calmly smoking cigarettes and gazing at nothing, with a look of ineffable contentment upon their features! They surely have solved the problem of life!"

But we seemed never to be able to free ourselves from the fetters of civilization, and so I struggled on.

One evening after dusk, I went into the kitchen, opened the kitchen closet door to take out some dish, when clatter! bang! down fell the bread-pan, and a shower of other tin ware, and before I could fairly get my breath, out jumped two young squaws and without deigning to glance at me they darted across the kitchen and leaped out the window like two frightened fawn.

They had on nothing but their birthday clothes and as I was somewhat startled at the sight of them, I stood transfixed, my eyes gazing at the open space through which they had flown.

Charley, the Indian, was in the corral, filling the *ollas*, and, hearing the commotion, came in and saw just the disappearing heels of the two squaws.

I said, very sternly: "Charley, how came those squaws in my closet?"

He looked very much ashamed and said: "Oh, me tell you: bad man go to kill 'em; I hide 'em."

"Well," said I, "do not hide any more girls in this *casa*! You savez that?"

He bowed his head in acquiescence.

I afterwards learned that one of the girls was his sister.

The weather was now fairly comfortable, and in the evenings we sat under the *ramada*, in front of the house, and watched the beautiful pink glow which spread over the entire heavens and illuminated the distant mountains of Lower California. I have never seen anything like that wonderful colour, which spread itself over sky, river and desert. For an hour, one could have believed oneself in a magician's realm.

At about this time, the sad-eyed Patrocina found it expedient to withdraw into the green valleys of Lower California, to recuperate for a few months. With the impish Jesusita in her arms, she bade me a mournful goodbye. Worthless as she was from the standpoint of civilized morals, I was attached to her and felt sorry to part with her.

Then I took a Mexican woman from Chihuahua. Now the Chihuahuans hold their heads high, and it was rather with awe that I greeted the tall middle-aged Chihuahuan lady who came to be our little son's nurse. Her name was Angela. "Angel of light," I thought, how fortunate I am to get her!

After a few weeks, Fisher observed that the whole village was eating Ferris ham, an unusual delicacy in Ehrenberg, and that the Goldwaters' had sold none. So he suggested that our commissary storehouse be looked to; and it was found that a dozen hams or so had been withdrawn from their canvas covers, the covers stuffed with straw, and hung back in place. Verily the Chihuahuan was adding to her pin-money in a most unworthy fashion, and she had to go. After that, I was left without a nurse. My little son was now about nine months old.

Milk began to be more plentiful at this season, and, with my sister's advice and help, I decided to make the one great change in a baby's life *i.e.*, to take him from his mother. Modern methods were unknown then, and we had neither of us any experience in these matters and there was no doctor in the place.

The result was, that both the baby and myself were painfully and desperately ill and not knowing which way to turn for aid, when, by a lucky turn of Fortune's wheel, our good, dear Doctor Henry Lippincott came through Ehrenberg on his way out to the States. Once more he took care of us, and it is to him that I believe I owe my life.

Captain Ernest sent us a cook from Yuma, and soon some officers came for the duck-shooting. There were thousands of ducks around the various lagoons in the neighbourhood, and the sport was rare. We had all the ducks we could eat.

Then came an earthquake, which tore and rent the baked earth apart. The ground shivered, the windows rattled, the birds fell close to the ground and could not fly, the stove-pipes fell to the floor, the thick walls cracked and finally, the earth rocked to and fro like some huge thing trying to get its balance.

It was in the afternoon. My sister and I were sitting with our needlework in the living-room. Little Harry was on the floor, occupied with some toys. I was paralyzed with fear; my sister did not move. We sat gazing at each other, scarce daring to breathe, expecting every instant the heavy walls to crumble about our heads. The earth rocked and rocked, and rocked again, then swayed and swayed and finally was still. My sister caught Harry in her arms, and then Jack and Willie came breathlessly in. "Did you feel it?" said Jack.

"Did we feel it!" said I, scornfully.

Sarah was silent, and I looked so reproachfully at Jack, that he dropped his light tone, and said: "It was pretty awful. We were in the Goldwaters' store, when suddenly it grew dark and the lamps above our heads began to rattle and swing, and we all rushed out into the middle of the street and stood, rather dazed, for we scarcely knew what had happened; then we hurried home. But it's all over now."

"I do not believe it," said I; "we shall have more"; and, in fact, we did have two light shocks in the night, but no more followed, and the next morning, we recovered, in a measure, from our fright and went out to see the great fissures in that treacherous crust of earth upon which Ehrenberg was built.

I grew afraid, after that, and the idea that the earth would eventually open and engulf us all took possession of my mind.

My health, already weakened by shocks and severe strains, gave way entirely. I, who had gloried in the most perfect health, and had a constitution of iron, became an emaciated invalid.

From my window, one evening at sundown, I saw a weird procession moving slowly along towards the outskirts of the village. It must be a funeral, thought I, and it flashed across my mind that I had never seen the burying-ground.

A man with a rude cross led the procession. Then came some Mexicans with violins and guitars. After the musicians, came the body of the deceased, wrapped in a white cloth, borne on a bier by friends, and followed by the little band of weeping women, with black *ribosos* folded about their heads. They did not use coffins at Ehrenberg, because they had none, I suppose.

The next day I asked Jack to walk to the grave-yard with me. He postponed it from day to day, but I insisted upon going. At last, he took me to see it.

There was no enclosure, but the bare, sloping, sandy place was sprinkled with graves, marked by heaps of stones, and in some instances by rude crosses of wood, some of which had been wrenched from their upright position by the fierce sand-storms. There was not a blade of grass, a tree, or a flower. I walked about among these graves, and close beside some of them I saw deep holes and whitened bones. I was quite ignorant or unthinking, and asked what the holes were.

"It is where the coyotes and wolves come in the nights," said Jack.

My heart sickened as I thought of these horrors, and I wondered if Ehrenberg held anything in store for me worse than what I had already seen. We turned away from this unhallowed grave-yard and walked to our quarters. I had never known much about "nerves," but I began to see spectres in the night, and those ghastly graves with their coyote-holes were ever before me. The place was but a stone's throw from us, and the uneasy spirits from these desecrated graves began to haunt me. I could not sit alone on the porch at night, for they peered through the lattice, and mocked at me, and beckoned. Some had no heads, some no arms, but they pointed or nodded towards the gruesome burying-ground: "You'll be with us soon, you'll be with us soon."

CHAPTER 22

Return to the States

I dream of the east wind's tonic,
Of the breakers' stormy roar,
And the peace of the inner harbour
With the long low Shimmo shore.
I long for the buoy-bell's tolling
When the north wind brings from afar
The smooth, green, shining billows,
To be churned into foam on the bar.
Oh! for the sea-gulls' screaming
As they swoop so bold and free!
Oh! for the fragrant commons,
And the glorious open sea!—
For the restful great contentment,
For the joy that is never known
Till past the jetty and Brant Point Light
The Islander comes to his own!
                              —Mary E. Starbuck.

"I must send you out. I see that you cannot stand it here another month," said Jack one day; and so he bundled us onto the
boat in the early spring, and took us down the river to meet the
ocean steamer.

There was no question about it this time, and I well knew
it.

I left my sister and her son in Ehrenberg, and I never saw
my nephew again. A month later, his state of health became so

alarming that my sister took him to San Francisco. He survived the long voyage, but died there a few weeks later at the home of my cousin.

At Fort Yuma we telegraphed all over the country for a nurse, but no money would tempt those Mexican women to face an ocean voyage. Jack put me on board the old *Newbern* in charge of the Captain, waited to see our vessel under way, then waved good-bye from the deck of the *Gila*, and turned his face towards his post and duty. I met the situation as best I could, and as I have already described a voyage on this old craft, I shall not again enter into details. There was no stewardess on board, and all arrangements were of the crudest description. Both my child and I were seasick all the way, and the voyage lasted sixteen days. Our misery was very great.

The passengers were few in number, only a couple of Mexican miners who had been prospecting, an irritable old Mexican woman, and a German doctor, who was agreeable but elusive.

The old Mexican woman sat on the deck all day, with her back against the stateroom door; she was a picturesque and indolent figure.

There was no diversion, no variety; my little boy required constant care and watching. The days seemed endless. Everybody bought great bunches of green bananas at the ports in Mexico, where we stopped for passengers.

The old woman was irritable, and one day when she saw the agreeable German doctor pulling bananas from the bunch which she had hung in the sun to ripen, she got up muttering "*Carramba*," and shaking her fist in his face. He appeased her wrath by offering her, in the most fluent Spanish, some from his own bunch when they should be ripe.

Such were my surroundings on the old *Newbern*. The German doctor was interesting, and I loved to talk with him, on days when I was not seasick, and to read the letters which he had received from his family, who were living on their Rittergut (or landed estates) in Prussia.

He amused me by tales of his life at a wretched little mining

139

village somewhere about fifty miles from Ehrenberg, and I was always wondering how he came to have lived there.

He had the keenest sense of humour, and as I listened to the tales of his adventures and miraculous escapes from death at the hands of these desperate folk, I looked in his large laughing blue eyes and tried to solve the mystery.

For that he was of noble birth and of ancient family there was no doubt. There were the letters, there was the crest, and here was the offshoot of the family. I made up my mind that he was a ne'er-do-weel and a rolling stone. He was elusive, and, beyond his adventures, told me nothing of himself. It was some time after my arrival in San Francisco that I learned more about him.

Now, after we rounded Cape St. Lucas, we were caught in the long heavy swell of the Pacific Ocean, and it was only at intervals that my little boy and I could leave our stateroom. The doctor often held him while I ran below to get something to eat, and I can never forget his kindness; and if, as I afterward heard in San Francisco, he really had entered the "Gate of a hundred sorrows," it would perhaps best explain his elusiveness, his general condition, and his sometimes dazed expression.

A gentle and kindly spirit, met by chance, known through the propinquity of a sixteen days' voyage, and never forgotten.

Everything comes to an end, however interminable it may seem, and at last the sharp and jagged outlines of the coast began to grow softer and we approached the Golden Gate.

The old *Newbern*, with nothing in her but ballast, rolled and lurched along, through the bright green waters of the outer bar. I stood leaning against the great mast, steadying myself as best I could, and the tears rolled down my face; for I saw the friendly green hills, and before me lay the glorious bay of San Francisco. I had left behind me the deserts, the black rocks, the burning sun, the snakes, the scorpions, the centipedes, the Indians and the Ehrenberg graveyard; and so the tears flowed, and I did not try to stop them; they were tears of joy.

The custom officers wanted to confiscate the great bundles of Mexican cigarettes they found in my trunk, but "No," I told them, "they were for my own use." They raised their eyebrows, gave me one look, and put them back into the trunk.

My beloved California relatives met us, and took care of us for a fortnight, and when I entered a Pullman car for a nine days' journey to my old home, it seemed like the most luxurious comfort, although I had a fourteen-months-old child in my arms, and no nurse. So does everything in this life go by comparison.

Arriving in Boston, my sister Harriet met me at the train, and as she took little Harry from my arms she cried: "Where did you get that sunbonnet? Now the baby can't wear that in Boston!"

Of course we were both thinking hard of all that had happened to me since we parted, on the morning after my wedding, two years before, and we were so overcome with the joy of meeting, that if it had not been for the baby's white sunbonnet, I do not know what kind of a scene we might have made. That saved the situation, and after a few days of rest and necessary shopping, we started for our old home in Nantucket. Such a welcome as the baby and I had from my mother and father and all old friends!

But I saw sadness in their faces, and I heard it in their voices, for no one thought I could possibly live. I felt, however, sure it was not too late. I knew the East wind's tonic would not fail me, its own child.

Stories of our experiences and misfortunes were eagerly listened to, by the family, and betwixt sighs and laughter they declared they were going to fill some boxes which should contain everything necessary for comfort in those distant places. So one room in our old house was set apart for this; great boxes were brought, and day by day various articles, useful, ornamental, and comfortable, and precious heirlooms of silver and glass, were packed away in them.

It was the year of 1876, the year of the great Centennial, at Philadelphia. Everybody went, but it had no attractions for me. I was happy enough, enjoying the health-giving air and the comforts of an Eastern home. I wondered that I had ever complained

141

about anything there, or wished to leave that blissful spot.

The poorest person in that place by the sea had more to be thankful for, in my opinion, than the richest people in Arizona. I felt as if I must cry it out from the house-tops. My heart was thankful every minute of the day and night, for every breath of soft air that I breathed, for every bit of fresh fish that I ate, for fresh vegetables, and for butter—for gardens, for trees, for flowers, for the good firm earth beneath my feet. I wrote the man on detached service that I should never return to Ehrenberg.

After eight months, in which my health was wholly restored, I heard the good news that Captain Corliss had applied for his first lieutenant, and I decided to join him at once at Camp Mac-Dowell.

Although I had not wholly forgotten that Camp MacDowell had been called by very bad names during our stay at Fort Whipple, at the time that Jack decided on the Ehrenberg detail, I determined to brave it, in all its unattractiveness, isolation and heat, for I knew there was a garrison and a Doctor there, and a few officers' families, I knew supplies were to be obtained and the ordinary comforts of a far-off post. Then too, in my summer in the East I had discovered that I was really a soldier's wife and I must go back to it all. To the army with its glitter and its misery, to the post with its discomforts, to the soldiers, to the drills, to the bugle-calls, to the monotony, to the heat of Southern Arizona, to the uniform and the stalwart Captains and gay Lieutenants who wore it, I felt the call and I must go.

CHAPTER 23

Back to Arizona

The last nails were driven in the precious boxes, and I started overland in November with my little son, now nearly two years old.

"Overland" in those days meant nine days from New York to San Francisco. Arriving in Chicago, I found it impossible to secure a section on the Pullman car so was obliged to content myself with a lower berth. I did not allow myself to be disappointed.

On entering the section, I saw an enormous pair of queer cow hide shoes, the very queerest shoes I had ever seen, lying on the floor, with a much used travelling bag. I speculated a good deal on the shoes, but did not see the owner of them until several hours later, when a short thick-set German with sandy close-cut beard entered and saluted me politely. "You are noticing my shoes perhaps *Madame?*"

"Yes" I said, involuntarily answering him in German.

His face shone with pleasure and he explained to me that they were made in Russia and he always wore them when travelling. "What have we," I thought, "an anarchist?"

But with the inexperience and fearlessness of youth, I entered into a most delightful conversation in German with him. I found him rather an extraordinarily well educated gentleman and he said he lived in Nevada, but had been over to Vienna to place his little boy at a military school, "as," he said, "there is nothing like a uniform to give a boy self-respect." He said his wife had died several months before. I congratulated myself that the occupant of the upper berth was at least a gentleman.

The next day, as we sat opposite each other chatting, always in German, he paused, and fixing his eyes rather steadily upon me he remarked: "Do you think I put on mourning when my wife died? no indeed, I put on white kid gloves and had a fiddler and danced at the grave. All this mourning that people have is utter nonsense."

I was amazed at the turn his conversation had taken and sat quite still, not knowing just what to say or to do.

After awhile, he looked at me steadily, and said, very deferentially, "*Madame*, the spirit of my dead wife is looking at me from out your eyes."

By this time I realized that the man was a maniac, and I had always heard that one must agree with crazy people, so I nodded, and that seemed to satisfy him, and bye and bye after some minutes which seemed like hours to me, he went off to the smoking room.

The tension was broken and I appealed to a very nice looking woman who happened to be going to some place in Nevada near which this doctor lived, and she said, when I told her his name, "Why, yes, I heard of him before I left home, he lives in Silver City, and at the death of his wife, he went hopelessly insane, but," she added, "he is harmless, I believe."

This was a nice fix, to be sure, and I staid over in her section all day, and late that night the doctor arrived at the junction where he was to take another train. So I slept in peace, after a considerable agitation.

There is nothing like experience to teach a young woman how to travel alone.

In San Francisco I learned that I could now go as far as Los Angeles by rail, thence by steamer to San Diego, and so on by stage to Fort Yuma, where my husband was to meet me with an ambulance and a wagon.

I was enchanted with the idea of avoiding the long sea-trip down the Pacific coast, but sent my boxes down by the Steamer

Montana, sister ship of the old *Newbern*, and after a few days' rest in San Francisco, set forth by rail for Los Angeles. At San Pedro, the port of Los Angeles, we embarked for San Diego. It was a heavenly night. I sat on deck enjoying the calm sea, and listening to the romantic story of Lieutenant Philip Reade, then stationed at San Diego. He was telling the story himself, and I had never read or heard of anything so mysterious or so tragic.

Then, too, aside from the story, Mr. Reade was a very good-looking and chivalrous young army officer. He was returning to his station in San Diego, and we had this pleasant opportunity to renew what had been a very slight acquaintance.

The calm waters of the Pacific, with their long and gentle swell, the pale light of the full moon, our steamer gliding so quietly along, the soft air of the California coast, the absence of noisy travellers, these made a fit setting for the story of his early love and marriage, and the tragic mystery which surrounded the death of his young bride.

All the romance which lived and will ever live in me was awake to the story, and the hours passed all too quickly.

But a cry from my little boy in the near-by deck stateroom recalled me to the realities of life and I said good-night, having spent one of the most delightful evenings I ever remember.

Mr. Reade wears now a star on his shoulder, and well earned it is, too. I wonder if he has forgotten how he helped to bind up my little boy's finger which had been broken in an accident on the train from San Francisco to Los Angeles? or how he procured a surgeon for me on our arrival there, and got a comfortable room for us at the hotel? or how he took us to drive (with an older lady for a chaperon), or how he kindly cared for us until we were safely on the boat that evening? If I had ever thought chivalry dead, I learned then that I had been mistaken.

San Diego charmed me, as we steamed, the next morning, into its shining bay. But as our boat was two hours late and the stage-coach was waiting, I had to decline Mr. Reade's enchanting offers to drive us around the beautiful place, to show me the fine beaches, and his quarters, and all other points of interest in this old town of Southern California.

Arizona, not San Diego, was my destination, so we took a hasty breakfast at the hotel and boarded the stage, which, filled with passengers, was waiting before the door.

The driver waited for no ceremonies, muttered something about being late, cracked his whip, and away we went. I tried to stow myself and my little boy and my belongings away comfortably, but the road was rough and the coach swayed, and I gave it up. There were passengers on top of the coach, and passengers inside the coach. One woman who was totally deaf, and some miners and blacksmiths, and a few other men, the flotsam and jetsam of the Western countries, who come from no one knoweth whence, and who go, no one knoweth whither, who have no trade or profession and are sometimes even without a name.

They seemed to want to be kind to me. Harry got very stagesick and gave us much trouble, and they all helped me to hold him. Night came. I do not remember that we made any stops at all; if we did, I have forgotten them. The night on that stagecoach can be better imagined than described. I do not know of any adjectives that I could apply to it. Just before dawn, we stopped to change horses and driver, and as the day began to break, we felt ourselves going down somewhere at a terrific speed.

The great Concord coach slipped and slid and swayed on its huge springs as we rounded the curves.

The road was narrow and appeared to be cut out of solid rock, which seemed to be as smooth as soapstone; the four horses were put to their speed, and down and around and away we went. I drew in my breath as I looked out and over into the abyss on my left. Death and destruction seemed to be the end awaiting us all. Everybody was limp, when we reached the bottom—that is, I was limp, and I suppose the others were. The stage-driver knew I was frightened, because I sat still and looked white and he came and lifted me out. He lived in a small cabin at the bottom of the mountain; I talked with him some. "The fact is," he said, "we are an hour late this morning; we always make it a point to 'do it' before dawn, so the passengers can't see anything; they are almost sure to get stampeded if we come down by daylight."

I mentioned this road afterwards in San Francisco, and learned that it was a famous road, cut out of the side of a solid mountain of rock; long talked of, long desired, and finally built, at great expense, by the state and the county together; that they always had the same man to drive over it, and that they never did it by daylight. I did not inquire if there had ever been any accidents. I seemed to have learned all I wanted to know about it.

After a little rest and a breakfast at a sort of roadhouse, a relay of horses was taken, and we travelled one more day over a flat country, to the end of the stage-route. Jack was to meet me. Already from the stage I had espied the post ambulance and two blue uniforms. Out jumped Major Ernest and Jack. I remember thinking how straight and how well they looked. I had forgotten really how army men did look, I had been so long away.

And now we were to go to Fort Yuma and stay with the Wells' until my boxes, which had been sent around by water on the steamer *Montana*, should arrive. I had only the usual thirty pounds allowance of luggage with me on the stage, and it was made up entirely of my boy's clothing, and an evening dress I had worn on the last night of my stay in San Francisco.

Fort Yuma was delightful at this season (December), and after four or five days spent most enjoyably, we crossed over one morning on the old rope ferryboat to Yuma City, to inquire at the big country store there of news from the Gulf. There was no bridge then over the Colorado.

The merchant called Jack to one side and said something to him in a low tone. I was sure it concerned the steamer, and I said: "what it is?"

Then they told me that news had just been received from below, that the *Montana* had been burned to the water's edge in Guaymas Harbor, and everything on board destroyed; the passengers had been saved with much difficulty, as the disaster occurred in the night.

I had lost all the clothes I had in the world—and my precious boxes were gone. I scarcely knew how to meet the calamity.

Jack said: "Don't mind, Mattie; I'm so thankful you and the boy were not on board the ship; the things are nothing, no account at all."

"But," said I, "you do not understand. I have no clothes except what I have on, and a party dress. Oh! what shall I do?" I cried.

The merchant was very sympathetic and kind, and Major Wells said, "Let's go home and tell Fanny; maybe she can suggest something."

I turned toward the counter, and bought some sewing materials, realizing that outside of my toilet articles and my party dress all my personal belongings were swept away. I was in a country where there were no dressmakers, and no shops; I was, for the time being, a pauper, as far as clothing was concerned.

When I got back to Mrs. Wells I broke down entirely; she put her arms around me and said: "I've heard all about it; I know just how you must feel; now come in my room, and we'll see what can be done."

She laid out enough clothing to last me until I could get some things from the East, and gave me a grey and white percale dress with a *basque*, and a border, and although it was all very much too large for me, it sufficed to relieve my immediate distress.

Letters were dispatched to the East, in various directions, for every sort and description of clothing, but it was at least two months before any of it appeared, and I felt like an object of charity for a long time. Then, too, I had anticipated the fitting up of our quarters with all the pretty *cretonnes* and other things I had brought from home. And now the contents of those boxes were no more! The memory of the visit was all that was left to me. It was very hard to bear.

Preparations for our journey to Camp MacDowell were at last completed. The route to our new post lay along the valley of the Gila River, following it up from its mouth, where it empties into the Colorado, eastwards towards the southern middle portion of Arizona.

CHAPTER 24

Up the Valley of the Gila

The December sun was shining brightly down, as only the Arizona sun can shine at high noon in winter, when we crossed the Colorado on the primitive ferryboat drawn by ropes, clambered up into the great thorough-brace wagon (or ambulance) with its dusty white canvas covers all rolled up at the sides, said good-bye to our kind hosts of Fort Yuma, and started, rattling along the sandy main street of Yuma City, for old Camp Mac-Dowell.

Our big blue army wagon, which had been provided for my boxes and trunks, rumbling along behind us, empty except for the camp equipage.

But it all seemed so good to me: I was happy to see the soldiers again, the drivers and teamsters, and even the sleek Government mules. The old blue uniforms made my heart glad. Every sound was familiar, even the rattling of the harness with its ivory rings and the harsh sound of the heavy brakes reinforced with old leather soles.

Even the country looked attractive, smiling under the December sun. I wondered if I had really grown to love the desert. I had read somewhere that people did. But I was not paying much attention in those days to the analysis of my feelings. I did not stop to question the subtle fascination which I felt steal over me as we rolled along the smooth hard roads that followed the windings of the Gila River. I was back again in the army; I had cast my lot with a soldier, and where he was, was home to me.

In Nantucket, no one thought much about the army. The uniform of the regulars was never seen there. The profession of arms was scarcely known or heard of. Few people manifested any interest in the life of the Far West. I had, while there, felt out of touch with my oldest friends. Only my darling old uncle, a brave old whaling captain, had said: "Mattie, I am much interested in all you have written us about Arizona; come right down below and show me on the dining-room map just where you went."

Gladly I followed him down the stairs, and he took his pencil out and began to trace. After he had crossed the Mississippi, there did not seem to be anything but blank country, and I could not find Arizona, and it was written in large letters across the entire half of this antique map, "Unexplored."

"True enough," he laughed. "I must buy me a new map."

But he drew his pencil around Cape Horn and up the Pacific coast, and I described to him the voyages I had made on the old *Newbern*, and his face was aglow with memories.

"Yes," he said, "in 1826, we put into San Francisco Harbor and sent our boats up to San Jose for water and we took goats from some of those islands, too. Oh! I know the coast well enough. We were on our way to the Ar'tic Ocean then, after right whales."

But, as a rule, people there seemed to have little interest in the army and it had made me feel as one apart.

Gila City was our first camp; not exactly a city, to be sure, at that time, whatever it may be now. We were greeted by the sight of a few old adobe houses, and the usual saloon. I had ceased, however, to dwell upon such trifles as names. Even "Filibuster," the name of our next camp, elicited no remark from me.

The weather was fine beyond description. Each day, at noon, we got out of the ambulance, and sat down on the warm white sand, by a little clump of mesquite, and ate our luncheon. Coveys of quail flew up and we shot them, thereby insuring a good supper.

The mules trotted along contentedly on the smooth white

road, which followed the south bank of the Gila River. Myriads of lizards ran out and looked at us. "Hello, here you are again," they seemed to say.

The Gila Valley in December was quite a different thing from the Mojave desert in September; and although there was not much to see, in that low, flat country, yet we three were joyous and happy.

Good health again was mine, the travelling was ideal, there were no discomforts, and I experienced no terrors in this part of Arizona.

Each morning, when the tent was struck, and I sat on the camp-stool by the little heap of ashes, which was all that remained of what had been so pleasant a home for an afternoon and a night, a little lonesome feeling crept over me, at the thought of leaving the place. So strong is the instinct and love of home in some people, that the little tendrils shoot out in a day and weave themselves around a spot which has given them shelter. Such as those are not born to be nomads.

Camps were made at Stanwix, Oatman's Flat, and Gila Bend. There we left the river, which makes a mighty loop at this point, and struck across the plains to Maricopa Wells. The last day's march took us across the Gila River, over the Maricopa desert, and brought us to the Salt River. We forded it at sundown, rested our animals a half hour or so, and drove through the MacDowell canon in the dark of the evening, nine miles more to the post. A day's march of forty-five miles. (A relay of mules had been sent to meet us at the Salt River, but by some oversight, we had missed it.)

Jack had told me of the curious *cholla* cactus, which is said to nod at the approach of human beings, and to deposit its barbed needles at their feet. Also I had heard stories of this deep, dark canon and things that had happened there.

Fort MacDowell was in Maricopa County, Arizona, on the Verde River, seventy miles or so south of Camp Verde; the roving bands of Indians, escaping from Camp Apache and the San Carlos reservation, which lay far to the east and southeast, often found secure hiding places in the fastnesses of the Superstition Mountains and other ranges, which lay between old Camp MacDowell and these reservations.

Hence, a company of cavalry and one of infantry were stationed at Camp MacDowell, and the officers and men of this small command were kept busy, scouting, and driving the renegades from out of this part of the country back to their reservations. It was by no means an idle post, as I found after I got there; the life at Camp MacDowell meant hard work, exposure and fatigue for this small body of men.

As we wound our way through this deep, dark canon, after crossing the Salt River, I remembered the things I had heard, of ambush and murder. Our animals were too tired to go out of a walk, the night fell in black shadows down between those high mountain walls, the *chollas*, which are a pale sage-green colour in the daytime, took on a ghastly hue. They were dotted here and there along the road, and on the steep mountainsides. They grew nearly as tall as a man, and on each branch were great excrescences which looked like people's heads, in the vague light which fell upon them.

They nodded to us, and it made me shudder; they seemed to be something human.

The soldiers were not partial to MacDowell canon; they knew too much about the place; and we all breathed a sigh of relief when we emerged from this dark uncanny road and saw the lights of the post, lying low, long, flat, around a square.

CHAPTER 25

Old Camp Macdowell

We were expected, evidently, for as we drove along the road in front of the officers' quarters they all came out to meet us, and we received a great welcome.

Captain Corliss of C company welcomed us to the post and to his company, and said he hoped I should like MacDowell better than I did Ehrenberg. Now Ehrenberg seemed years agone, and I could laugh at the mention of it.

Supper was awaiting us at Captain Corliss's, and Mrs. Kendall, wife of Lieutenant Kendall, Sixth Cavalry, had, in Jack's absence, put the finishing touches to our quarters. So I went at once to a comfortable home, and life in the army began again for me.

How good everything seemed! There was Doctor Clark, whom I had met first at Ehrenberg, and who wanted to throw Patrocina and Jesusita into the Colorado. I was so glad to find him there; he was such a good doctor, and we never had a moment's anxiety, as long as he staid at Camp MacDowell. Our confidence in him was unbounded.

It was easy enough to obtain a man from the company. There were then no hateful laws forbidding soldiers to work in officers' families; no dreaded inspectors, who put the flat question, "Do you employ a soldier for menial labour?"

Captain Corliss gave me an old man by the name of Smith, and he was glad to come and stay with us and do what simple cooking we required. One of the laundresses let me have her daughter for nursery-maid, and our small establishment at

Camp MacDowell moved on smoothly, if not with elegance.

The officers' quarters were a long, low line of adobe buildings with no space between them; the houses were separated only by thick walls. In front, the windows looked out over the parade ground. In the rear, they opened out on a road which ran along the whole length, and on the other side of which lay another row of long, low buildings which were the kitchens, each set of quarters having its own.

We occupied the quarters at the end of the row, and a large bay window looked out over a rather desolate plain, and across to the large and well-kept hospital. As all my draperies and pretty cretonnes had been burnt up on the ill-fated ship, I had nothing but bare white shades at the windows, and the rooms looked desolate enough. But a long divan was soon built, and some coarse yellow cotton bought at John Smith's (the cutler's) store, to cover it. My pretty rugs and mats were also gone, and there was only the old ingrain carpet from Fort Russell.

The floors were *adobe*, and some men from the company came and laid down old canvas, then the carpet, and drove in great spikes around the edge to hold it down. The floors of the bedroom and dining-room were covered with canvas in the same manner. Our furnishings were very scanty and I felt very mournful about the loss of the boxes. We could not claim restitution as the steamship company had been courteous enough to take the boxes down free of charge.

John Smith, the post trader (the name "sutler" fell into disuse about now) kept a large store but, nothing that I could use to beautify my quarters with—and our losses had been so heavy that we really could not afford to send back East for more things. My new white dresses came and were suitable enough for the winter climate of MacDowell. But I missed the thousand and one accessories of a woman's wardrobe, the accumulation of years, the comfortable things which money could not buy especially at that distance.

I had never learned how to make dresses or to fit garments and although I knew how to sew, my accomplishments ran more in the line of outdoor sports.

But Mrs. Kendall whose experience in frontier life had made her self-reliant, lent me some patterns, and I bought some of John Smith's calico and went to work to make gowns suited to the hot weather. This was in 1877, and every one will remember that the ready-made house-gowns were not to be had in those days in the excellence and profusion in which they can to-day be found, in all parts of the country.

Now Mrs. Kendall was a tall, fine woman, much larger than I, but I used her patterns without alterations, and the result was something like a bag. They were freshly laundried and cool, however, and I did not place so much importance on the lines of them, as the young women of the present time do. Today, the poorest farmer's wife in the wilds of Arkansas or Alaska can wear better fitting gowns than I wore then. But my riding habits, of which I had several kinds, to suit warm and cold countries, had been left in Jack's care at Ehrenberg, and as long as these fitted well, it did not so much matter about the gowns.

Captain Chaffee, who commanded the company of the Sixth Cavalry stationed there, was away on leave, but Mr. Kendall, his first lieutenant, consented for me to exercise "Cochise," Captain Chaffee's Indian pony, and I had a royal time.

Cavalry officers usually hate riding: that is, riding for pleasure; for they are in the saddle so much, for dead earnest work; but a young officer, a second lieutenant, not long out from the Academy, liked to ride, and we had many pleasant riding parties. Mr. Dravo and I rode one day to the Mormon settlement, seventeen miles away, on some business with the bishop, and a Mormon woman gave us a lunch of fried salt pork, potatoes, bread, and milk.

How good it tasted, after our long ride! and how we laughed about it all, and jollied, after the fashion of young people, all the way back to the post! Mr Dravo had also lost all his things on the "Montana," and we sympathized greatly with each other. He, however, had sent an order home to Pennsylvania, duplicating all the contents of his boxes. I told him I could not duplicate mine, if I sent a thousand orders East.

When, after some months, his boxes came, he brought me in a package, done up in tissue paper and tied with ribbon: "Mother sends you these; she wrote that I was not to open them; I think she felt sorry for you, when I wrote her you had lost all your clothing. I suppose," he added, mustering his West Point French to the front, and handing me the package, "it is what you ladies call 'lingerie.'"

I hope I blushed, and I think I did, for I was not so very old, and I was touched by this sweet remembrance from the dear mother back in Pittsburgh. And so many lovely things happened all the time; everybody was so kind to me. Mrs. Kendall and her young sister, Kate Taylor, Mrs. John Smith and I, were the only women that winter at Camp MacDowell. Afterwards, Captain Corliss brought a bride to the post, and a new doctor took Doctor Clark's place.

There were interminable scouts, which took both cavalry and infantry out of the post. We heard a great deal about "chasing Injuns" in the Superstition Mountains, and once a lieutenant of infantry went out to chase an escaping Indian Agent.

Old Smith, my cook, was not very satisfactory; he drank a good deal, and I got very tired of the trouble he caused me. It was before the days of the canteen, and soldiers could get all the whiskey they wanted at the trader's store; and, it being generally the brand that was known in the army as "Forty rod," they got very drunk on it sometimes. I never had it in my heart to blame them much, poor fellows, for every human beings wants and needs some sort of recreation and jovial excitement.

Captain Corliss said to Jack one day, in my presence, "I had a fine batch of recruits come in this morning."

"That's lovely," said I; "what kind of men are they? Any good cooks amongst them?" (for I was getting very tired of Smith).

Captain Corliss smiled a grim smile. "What do you think the United States Government enlists men for?" said he; "do you think I want my company to be made up of dish-washers?"

He was really quite angry with me, and I concluded that I

had been too abrupt, in my eagerness for another man, and that my ideas on the subject were becoming warped. I decided that I must be more diplomatic in the future, in my dealings with the Captain of C company.

The next day, when we went to breakfast, whom did we find in the dining-room but Bowen! Our old Bowen of the long march across the Territory! Of Camp Apache and K company! He had his white apron on, his hair rolled back in his most fetching style, and was putting the coffee on the table.

"But, Bowen," said I, "where—how on earth—did you-how did you know we—what does it mean?"

Bowen saluted the first lieutenant of C company, and said: "Well, sir, the fact is, my time was out, and I thought I would quit. I went to San Francisco and worked in a miners' restaurant" (here he hesitated), "but I didn't like it, and I tried something else, and lost all my money, and I got tired of the town, so I thought I'd take on again, and as I knowed ye's were in C company now, I thought I'd come to MacDowell, and I came over here this morning and told old Smith he'd better quit; this was my job, and here I am, and I hope ye're all well—and the little boy?"

Here was loyalty indeed, and here was Bowen the Immortal, back again!

And now things ran smoothly once more. Roasts of beef and haunches of venison, ducks and other good things we had through the winter.

It was cool enough to wear white cotton dresses, but nothing heavier. It never rained, and the climate was superb, although it was always hot in the sun. We had heard that it was very hot here; in fact, people called MacDowell by very bad names. As the spring came on, we began to realize that the epithets applied to it might be quite appropriate.

In front of our quarters was a *ramada*, [1] supported by rude poles of the cottonwood tree. Then came the sidewalk, and the *acequia* (ditch), then a row of young cottonwood trees, then the

---

1. A sort of rude awning made of brush and supported by cottonwood poles.

parade ground. Through the *acequia* ran the clear water that supplied the post, and under the shade of the *ramadas*, hung the large *ollas* from which we dipped the drinking water, for as yet, of course, ice was not even dreamed of in the far plains of Mac-Dowell. The heat became intense, as the summer approached. To sleep inside the house was impossible, and we soon followed the example of the cavalry, who had their beds out on the parade ground.

Two iron cots, therefore, were brought from the hospital, and placed side by side in front of our quarters, beyond the *acequia* and the cottonwood trees, in fact, out in the open space of the parade ground. Upon these were laid some mattresses and sheets, and after "taps" had sounded, and lights were out, we retired to rest. Near the cots stood Harry's crib. We had not thought about the ants, however, and they swarmed over our beds, driving us into the house.

The next morning Bowen placed a tin can of water under each point of contact; and as each cot had eight legs, and the crib had four, twenty cans were necessary. He had not taken the trouble to remove the labels, and the pictures of red tomatoes glared at us in the hot sun through the day; they did not look poetic, but our old enemies, the ants, were outwitted.

There was another species of tiny insect, however, which seemed to drop from the little cotton-wood trees which grew at the edge of the *acequia*, and myriads of them descended and crawled all over us, so we had to have our beds moved still farther out on to the open space of the parade ground.

And now we were fortified against all the venomous creeping things and we looked forward to blissful nights of rest.

We did not look along the line, when we retired to our cots, but if we had, we should have seen shadowy figures, laden with pillows, flying from the houses to the cots or vice versa. It was certainly a novel experience.

With but a sheet for a covering, there we lay, looking up at the starry heavens. I watched the Great Bear go around, and other constellations and seemed to come into close touch with

Nature and the mysterious night. But the melancholy solemnity of my communings was much affected by the howling of the coyotes, which seemed sometimes to be so near that I jumped to the side of the crib, to see if my little boy was being carried off. The good sweet slumber which I craved never came to me in those weird Arizona nights under the stars.

At about midnight, a sort of dewy coolness would come down from the sky, and we could then sleep a little; but the sun rose incredibly early in that southern country, and by the crack of dawn sheeted figures were to be seen darting back into the quarters, to try for another nap. The nap rarely came to any of us, for the heat of the houses never passed off, day or night, at that season. After an early breakfast, the long day began again.

The question of what to eat came to be a serious one. We experimented with all sorts of tinned foods, and tried to produce some variety from them, but it was all rather tiresome. We almost dreaded the visits of the paymaster and the inspector at that season, as we never had anything in the house to give them.

One hot night, at about ten o'clock, we heard the rattle of wheels, and an ambulance drew up at our door. Out jumped Colonel Biddle, Inspector General, from Fort Whipple. "What shall I give him to eat, poor hungry man?" I thought. I looked in the wire-covered safe, which hung outside the kitchen, and discovered half a beefsteak-pie. The gallant colonel declared that if there was one thing above all others that he liked, it was cold beefsteak-pie. Lieutenant Thomas of the Fifth Cavalry echoed his sentiments, and with a bottle of Cocomonga, which was always kept cooling somewhere, they had a merry supper.

These visits broke the monotony of our life at Camp Mac-Dowell. We heard of the gay doings up at Fort Whipple, and of the lovely climate there.

Mr. Thomas said he could not understand why we wore such bags of dresses. I told him spitefully that if the women of Fort Whipple would come down to MacDowell to spend the summer, they would soon be able to explain it to him. I began to feel embarrassed at the fit of my house-gowns. After a few days spent with us, however, the mercury ranging from 104 to 120 degrees in the shade, he ceased to comment upon our dresses or our customs.

I had a glass jar of butter sent over from the commissary, and asked Colonel Biddle if he thought it right that such butter as that should be bought by the purchasing officer in San Francisco. It had melted, and separated into layers of dead white, deep orange and pinkish-purple colours. Thus I, too, as well as General Miles, had my turn at trying to reform the Commissary Department of Uncle Sam's army.

Hammocks were swung under the *ramadas*, and after luncheon everybody tried a *siesta*. Then, near sundown, an ambulance came and took us over to the Verde River, about a mile away, where we bathed in water almost as thick as that of the Great Colorado. We taught Mrs. Kendall to swim, but Mr. Kendall, being an inland man, did not take to the water. Now the Verde River was not a very good substitute for the sea, and the thick water filled our ears and mouths, but it gave us a little half hour in the day when we could experience a feeling of being cool, and we found it worthwhile to take the trouble. Thick clumps of mesquite trees furnished us with dressing-rooms. We were all young, and youth requires so little with which to make merry.

After the meagre evening dinner, the Kendalls and ourselves sat together under the *ramada* until taps, listening generally to the droll anecdotes told by Mr. Kendall, who had an inexhaustible fund. Then another night under the stars, and so passed the time away.

We lived, ate, slept by the bugle calls. Reveille means sunrise, when a lieutenant must hasten to put himself into uniform, sword and belt, and go out to receive the report of the company or companies of soldiers, who stand drawn up in line on the parade ground.

At about nine o'clock in the morning comes the guardmount, a function always which everybody goes out to see. Then the various drill calls, and recalls, and sick-call and the beautiful stable-call for the cavalry, when the horses are groomed and watered, the thrilling fire-call and the startling assembly, or call-to-arms, when every soldier jumps for his rifle and every officer buckles on his sword, and a woman's heart stands still.

Then at night, "tattoo," when the company officers go out to receive the report of "all present and accounted for"—and shortly after that, the mournful "taps," a signal for the barrack lights to be put out.

The bugle call of "taps" is mournful also through association, as it is always blown over the grave of a soldier or an officer, after the coffin has been lowered into the earth. The soldier-musicians who blow the calls, seem to love the call of "taps," (strangely enough) and I remember well that there at Camp MacDowell, we all used to go out and listen when "taps went," as the soldier who blew it, seemed to put a whole world of sorrow into it, turning to the four points of the compass and letting its clear tones tremble through the air, away off across the Maricopa desert and then toward the East, our home so far away. We never spoke, we just listened, and who can tell the thoughts that each one had in his mind? Church nor ministers nor priests had we there in those distant lands, but can we say that our lives were wholly without religion?

The Sunday inspection of men and barracks, which was performed with much precision and formality, and often in full dress uniform, gave us something by which we could mark the weeks, as they slipped along. There was no religious service of any kind, as Uncle Sam did not seem to think that the souls of us people in the outposts needed looking after. It would have afforded much comfort to the Roman Catholics had there been a priest stationed there.

The only sermon I ever heard in old Camp MacDowell was delivered by a Mormon Bishop and was of a rather preposterous nature, neither instructive nor edifying. But the good Catholics read their prayer-books at home, and the rest of us almost forgot that such organizations as churches existed.

Another bright winter found us still gazing at the Four Peaks of the MacDowell Mountains, the only landmark on the horizon. I was glad, in those days, that I had not staid back East, for the life of an officer without his family, in those drear places, is indeed a blank and empty one.

"Four years I have sat here and looked at the Four Peaks," said Captain Corliss, one day, "and I'm getting almighty tired of it."

CHAPTER 26

A Sudden Order

In June, 1878, Jack was ordered to report to the commanding officer at Fort Lowell (near the ancient city of Tucson), to act as quartermaster and commissary at that post. This was a sudden and totally unexpected order. It was indeed hard, and it seemed to me cruel. For our regiment had been four years in the Territory, and we were reasonably sure of being ordered out before long. Tucson lay far to the south of us, and was even hotter than this place. But there was nothing to be done; we packed up, I with a heavy heart, Jack with his customary stoicism.

With the grief which comes only at that time in one's life, and which sees no end and no limit, I parted from my friends at Camp MacDowell. Two years together, in the most intimate companionship, cut off from the outside world, and away from all early ties, had united us with indissoluble bonds,—and now we were to part,—forever as I thought.

We all wept; I embraced them all, and Jack lifted me into the ambulance; Mrs. Kendall gave a last kiss to our little boy; Donahue, our soldier-driver, loosened up his brakes, cracked his long whip, and away we went, down over the flat, through the dark MacDowell canon, with the *chollas* nodding to us as we passed, across the Salt River, and on across an open desert to Florence, forty miles or so to the southeast of us.

At Florence we sent our military transportation back and staid over a day at a tavern to rest. We met there a very agreeable and cultivated gentleman, Mr. Charles Poston, who was *en route* to his home, somewhere in the mountains nearby. We took the Tucson stage at sundown, and travelled all night. I heard afterwards more about Mr. Poston: he had attained some reputation in the literary world by writing about the Sun-worshippers of Asia.

He had been a great traveller in his early life, but now had built himself some sort of a house in one of the desolate mountains which rose out of these vast plains of Arizona, hoisted his sun-flag on the top, there to pass the rest of his days. People out there said he was a sun-worshipper. I do not know. "But when I am tired of life and people," I thought, "this will not be the place I shall choose."

Arriving at Tucson, after a hot and tiresome night in the stage, we went to an old hostelry. Tucson looked attractive. Ancient civilization is always interesting to me.

Leaving me at the tavern, my husband drove out to Fort Lowell, to see about quarters and things in general. In a few hours he returned with the overwhelming news that he found a dispatch awaiting him at that post, ordering him to return immediately to his company at Camp MacDowell, as the Eighth Infantry was ordered to the Department of California.

Ordered "out" at last! I felt like jumping up onto the table, climbing onto the roof, dancing and singing and shouting for joy! Tired as we were (and I thought I had reached the limit), we were not too tired to take the first stage back for Florence, which left that evening. Those two nights on the Tucson stage are a blank in my memory. I got through them somehow.

In the morning, as we approached the town of Florence, the great blue army wagon containing our household goods, hove in sight—its white canvas cover stretched over hoops, its six sturdy mules coming along at a good trot, and Sergeant Stone cracking his long whip, to keep up a proper pace in the eyes of the Tucson stage-driver.

Jack called him to halt, and down went the sergeant's big brakes. Both teams came to a standstill, and we told the sergeant the news. Bewilderment, surprise, joy, followed each other on the old sergeant's countenance. He turned his heavy team about, and promised to reach Camp MacDowell as soon as the animals could make it.

At Florence, we left the stage, and went to the little tavern once more; the stage route did not lie in our direction, so we must hire a private conveyance to bring us to Camp MacDowell. Jack found a man who had a good pair of ponies and an open buckboard. Towards night we set forth to cross the plain which lies between Florence and the Salt River, due northwest by the map.

When I saw the driver I did not care much for his appearance. He did not inspire me with confidence, but the ponies looked strong, and we had forty or fifty miles before us.

After we got fairly into the desert, which was a trackless waste, I became possessed by a feeling that the man did not know the way. He talked a good deal about the North Star, and the fork in the road, and that we must be sure not to miss it.

It was a still, hot, starlit night. Jack and the driver sat on the front seat. They had taken the back seat out, and my little boy and I sat in the bottom of the wagon, with the hard cushions to lean against through the night. I suppose we were drowsy with sleep; at all events, the talk about the fork of the road and the North Star faded away into dreams.

I awoke with a chilly feeling, and a sudden jolt over a rock. "I do not recollect any rocks on this road, Jack, when we came over it in the ambulance," said I.

"Neither do I," he replied.

I looked for the North Star: I had looked for it often when in open boats. It was away off on our left, the road seemed to be ascending and rocky: I had never seen this piece of road before, that I was sure of.

"We are going to the eastward," said I, "and we should be going northwest."

"My dear, lie down and go to sleep; the man knows the road; he is taking a short cut, I suppose," said the Lieutenant. There was something not at all reassuring in his tones, however.

The driver did not turn his head nor speak. I looked at the North Star, which was getting farther and farther on our left, and I felt the gloomy conviction that we were lost on the desert.

Finally, at daylight, after going higher and higher, we drew up in an old deserted mining-camp.

The driver jerked his ponies up, and, with a sullen gesture, said, "We must have missed the fork of the road; this is Picket Post."

"Great Heavens!" I cried; "how far out of the way are we?"

"About fifteen miles," he drawled, "you see we shall have to go back to the place where the road forks, and make a new start."

I nearly collapsed with discouragement. I looked around at the ruined walls and crumbling pillars of stone, so weird and so grey in the dawning light: it might have been a worshipping place of the Druids. My little son shivered with the light chill which comes at daybreak in those tropical countries: we were hungry and tired and miserable: my bones ached, and I felt like crying.

We gave the poor ponies time to breathe, and took a bite of cold food ourselves.

Ah! that blighted and desolate place called Picket Post! Forsaken by God and man, it might have been the entrance to Hades.

Would the ponies hold out? They looked jaded to be sure, but we had stopped long enough to breathe them, and away they trotted again, down the mountain this time, instead of up.

It was broad day when we reached the fork of the road, which we had not been able to see in the night: there was no mistaking it now.

We had travelled already about forty miles, thirty more lay before us; but there were no hills, it was all flat country, and the owner of these brave little ponies said we could make it.

As we neared the MacDowell canon, we met Captain Corliss marching out with his company (truly they had lost no time in starting for California), and he told his first lieutenant he would make slow marches, that we might overtake him before he reached Yuma.

We were obliged to wait at Camp MacDowell for Sergeant Stone to arrive with our wagonful of household goods, and then, after a mighty weeding out and repacking, we set forth once more, with a good team of mules and a good driver, to join the command. We bade the Sixth Cavalry people once more goodbye, but I was so nearly dead by this time, with the heat, and the fatigue of all this hard travelling and packing up, that the keener edge of my emotions was dulled. Eight days and nights spent in travelling hither and thither over those hot plains in Southern Arizona, and all for what?

Because somebody in ordering somebody to change his station, had forgotten that somebody's regiment was about to be ordered out of the country it had been in for four years. Also because my husband was a soldier who obeyed orders without questioning them. If he had been a political wire-puller, many of our misfortunes might have been averted. But then, while I half envied the wives of the wire-pullers, I took a sort of pride in the blind obedience shown by my own particular soldier to the orders he received.

After that week's experience, I held another colloquy with myself, and decided that wives should not follow their husbands in the army, and that if I ever got back East again, I would stay: I simply could not go on enduring these unmitigated and unreasonable hardships.

The Florence man staid over at the post a day or so to rest his ponies. I bade him good-bye and told him to take care of those brave little beasts, which had travelled seventy miles without rest, to bring us to our destination. He nodded pleasantly and drove away. "A queer customer," I observed to Jack.

"Yes," answered he, "they told me in Florence that he was a 'road agent' and desperado, but there did not seem to be anyone else, and my orders were peremptory, so I took him. I knew the ponies could pull us through, by the looks of them; and road agents are all right with army officers, they know they wouldn't get anything if they held 'em up."

"How much did he charge you for the trip?" I asked.

"Sixteen dollars," was the reply. And so ended the episode. Except that I looked back to Picket Post with a sort of horror, I thought no more about it.

CHAPTER 27

The Eighth Foot Leaves Arizona

And now after the eight days of most distressing heat, and the fatigue of all sorts and varieties of travelling, the nights spent in a stage-coach or at a desert inn, or in the road agent's buckboard, holding always my little son close to my side, came six days more of journeying down the valley of the Gila.

We took supper in Phoenix, at a place known as "Devine's." I was hearing a good deal about Phoenix; for even then, its gardens, its orchards and its climate were becoming famous, but the season of the year was unpropitious to form a favourable opinion of that thriving place, even if my opinions of Arizona, with its parched-up soil and insufferable heat, had not been formed already.

We crossed the Gila somewhere below there, and stopped at our old camping places, but the entire valley was seething hot, and the remembrance of the December journey seemed but an aggravating dream.

We joined Captain Corliss and the company at Antelope Station, and in two more days were at Yuma City. By this time, the Southern Pacific Railroad had been built as far as Yuma, and a bridge thrown across the Colorado at this point. It seemed an incongruity. And how burning hot the cars looked, standing there in the Arizona sun!

After four years in that Territory, and remembering the days, weeks, and even months spent in travelling on the river, or marching through the deserts, I could not make the Pullman cars seem a reality.

We brushed the dust of the Gila Valley from our clothes, I unearthed a hat from somewhere, and some wraps which had not seen the light for nearly two years, and prepared to board the train.

I cried out in my mind, the prayer of the woman in one of Fisher's Ehrenberg stories, to which I used to listen with unmitigated delight, when I lived there. The story was this: "Mrs. Blank used to live here in Ehrenberg; she hated the place just as you do, but she was obliged to stay. Finally, after a period of two years, she and her sister, who had lived with her, were able to get away. I crossed over the river with them to Lower California, on the old rope ferry-boat which they used to have near Ehrenberg, and as soon as the boat touched the bank, they jumped ashore, and down they both went upon their knees, clasped their hands, raised their eyes to Heaven, and Mrs. Blank said: 'I thank Thee, oh Lord! Thou hast at last delivered us from the wilderness, and brought us back to God's country. Receive my thanks, oh Lord!'"

And then Fisher used to add: "And the tears rolled down their faces, and I knew they felt every word they spoke; and I guess you'll feel about the same way when you get out of Arizona, even if you don't quite drop on your knees," he said.

The soldiers did not look half so picturesque, climbing into the cars, as they did when loading onto a barge; and when the train went across the bridge, and we looked down upon the swirling red waters of the Great Colorado from the windows of a luxurious Pullman, I sighed; and, with the strange contradictoriness of the human mind, I felt sorry that the old days had come to an end. For, somehow, the hardships and deprivations which we have endured, lose their bitterness when they have become only a memory.

CHAPTER 28

California and Nevada

A portion of our regiment was ordered to Oregon, to join General Howard, who was conducting the Bannock Campaign, so I remained that summer in San Francisco, to await my husband's return.

I could not break away from my Arizona habits. I wore only white dresses, partly because I had no others which were in fashion, partly because I had become imbued with a profound indifference to dress.

"They'll think you're a Mexican," said my New England aunt (who regarded all foreigners with contempt). "Let them think," said I; "I almost wish I were; for, after all, they are the only people who understand the philosophy of living. Look at the tired faces of the women in your streets," I added, "one never sees that sort of expression down below, and I have made up my mind not to be caught by the whirlpool of advanced civilization again."

Added to the white dresses, I smoked cigarettes, and slept all the afternoons. I was in the bondage of tropical customs, and I had lapsed back into a state of what my aunt called semi-barbarism.

"Let me enjoy this heavenly cool climate, and do not worry me," I begged. I shuddered when I heard people complain of the cold winds of the San Francisco summer. How do they dare tempt Fate, thought I, and I wished them all in Ehrenberg or MacDowell for one summer. "I think they might then know something about climate, and would have something to complain about!"

How I revelled in the flowers, and all the luxuries of that delightful city!

The headquarters of the Eighth was located at Benicia, and General Kautz, our Colonel, invited me to pay a visit to his wife. A pleasant boat-trip up the Sacramento River brought us to Benicia. Mrs. Kautz, a handsome and accomplished Austrian, presided over her lovely army home in a manner to captivate my fancy, and the luxury of their surroundings almost made me speechless.

"The other side of army life," thought I.

A visit to Angel Island, one of the harbour defences, strengthened this impression. Four years of life in the southern posts of Arizona had almost made me believe that army life was indeed but "glittering misery," as the Germans had called it.

In the autumn, the troops returned from Oregon, and C company was ordered to Camp MacDermit, a lonely spot up in the northern part of Nevada (Nevada being included in the Department of California). I was sure by that time that bad luck was pursuing us. I did not know so much about the "ins and outs" of the army then as I do now.

At my aunt's suggestion, I secured a Chinaman of good caste for a servant, and by deceiving him (also my aunt's advice) with the idea that we were going only as far as Sacramento, succeeded in making him willing to accompany us.

We started east, and left the railroad at a station called "Winnemucca." MacDermit lay ninety miles to the north. But at Winnemucca the Chinaman balked. "You say: 'All'e same Saclamento': lis place heap too far: me no likee!" I talked to him, and, being a good sort, he saw that I meant well, and the soldiers bundled him on top of the army wagon, gave him a lot of good-natured guying, and a revolver to keep off Indians, and so we secured Hoo Chack.

Captain Corliss had been obliged to go on ahead with his wife, who was in the most delicate health. The post ambulance had met them at this place.

Jack was to march over the ninety miles, with the company. I watched them starting out, the men, glad of the release from the railroad train, their guns on their shoulders, stepping off in military style and in good form.

The wagons followed—the big blue army wagons, and Hoo Chack, looking rather glum, sitting on top of a pile of baggage.

I took the Silver City stage, and except for my little boy I was the only passenger for the most of the way. We did the ninety miles without resting over, except for relays of horses.

I climbed up on the box and talked with the driver. I liked these stage-drivers. They were "nervy," fearless men, and kind, too, and had a great dash and go about them. They often had a quiet and gentle bearing, but by that time I knew pretty well what sort of stuff they were made of, and I liked to have them talk to me, and I liked to look out upon the world through their eyes, and judge of things from their standpoint.

It was an easy journey, and we passed a comfortable night in the stage.

Camp MacDermit was a colourless, forbidding sort of a place. Only one company was stationed there, and my husband was nearly always scouting in the mountains north of us. The weather was severe, and the winter there was joyless and lonesome. The extreme cold and the loneliness affected my spirits, and I suffered from depression.

I had no woman to talk to, for Mrs. Corliss, who was the only other officer's wife at the post, was confined to the house by the most delicate health, and her mind was wholly absorbed by the care of her young infant. There were no nurses to be had in that desolate corner of the earth.

One day, a dreadful looking man appeared at the door, a person such as one never sees except on the outskirts of civilization, and I wondered what business brought him. He wore a long, black, greasy frock coat, a tall hat, and had the face of a sneak. He wanted the Chinaman's poll-tax, he said.

"But," I suggested, "I never heard of collecting taxes in a Government post; soldiers and officers do not pay taxes."

"That may be," he replied, "but your Chinaman is not a soldier, and I am going to have his tax before I leave this house."

"So, ho," I thought; "a threat!" and the soldier's blood rose in me.

I was alone; Jack was miles away up North. Hoo Chack appeared in the hall; he had evidently heard the man's last remark. "Now," I said, "this Chinaman is in my employ, and he shall not pay any tax, until I find out if he be exempt or not."

The evil-looking man approached the Chinaman. Hoo Chack grew a shade paler. I fancied he had a knife under his white shirt; in fact, he felt around for it. I said, "Hoo Chack, go away, I will talk to this man."

I opened the front door. "Come with me" (to the tax-collector); "we will ask the commanding officer about this matter." My heart was really in my mouth, but I returned the man's steady and dogged gaze, and he followed me to Captain Corliss' quarters. I explained the matter to the captain, and left the man to his mercy. "Why didn't you call the sergeant of the Guard, and have the man slapped into the guard-house?" said Jack, when I told him about it afterwards. "The man had no business around here; he was trying to browbeat you into giving him a dollar, I suppose."

The country above us was full of desperadoes from Boise and Silver City, and I was afraid to be left alone so much at night; so I begged Captain Corliss to let me have a soldier to sleep in my quarters. He sent me old Needham. So I installed old Needham in my guest chamber with his loaded rifle. Now old Needham was but a wisp of a man; long years of service had broken down his health; he was all wizened up and feeble; but he was a soldier; I felt safe, and could sleep once more. Just the sight of Needham and his old blue uniform coming at night, after taps, was a comfort to me.

Anxiety filled my soul, for Jack was scouting in the Stein Mountains all winter in the snow, after Indians who were avowedly hostile, and had threatened to kill on sight. He often went out with a small pack-train, and some Indian scouts, five or six soldiers, and I thought it quite wrong for him to be sent into the mountains with so small a number.

Camp MacDermit was, as I have already mentioned, a "one-company post." We all know what that may mean, on the frontier. Our Second Lieutenant was absent, and all the hard work of winter scouting fell upon Jack, keeping him away for weeks at a time.

The Piute Indians were supposed to be peaceful, and their old chief, Winnemucca, once the warlike and dreaded foe of the white man, was now quiet enough, and too old to fight. He lived, with his family, at an Indian village near the post.

He came to see me occasionally. His dress was a curious mixture of civilization and savagery. He wore the *chapeau* and dress-coat of a General of the American Army, with a large epaulette on one shoulder. He was very proud of the coat, because General Crook had given it to him. His shirt, leggings and moccasins were of buckskin, and the long braids of his coal-black hair, tied with strips of red flannel, gave the last touch to this incongruous costume.

But I must say that his demeanour was gentle and dignified, and, after recovering from the superficial impressions which his startling costume had at first made upon my mind, I could well believe that he had once been the war-leader, as he was now the political head of his once-powerful tribe.

Winnemucca did not disdain to accept some little sugar-cakes from me, and would sit down on our veranda and munch them.

He always showed me the pasteboard medal which hung around his neck, and which bore General Howard's signature; and he always said: "General Howard tell me, me good Injun, me go up—up—up"—pointing dramatically towards Heaven. On one occasion, feeling desperate for amusement, I said to him: "General Howard very good man, but he make a mistake; where you go, is not up—up—up, but," pointing solemnly to the earth below us, "down—down—down." He looked incredulous, but I assured him it was a nice place down there.

Some of the scattered bands of the tribe, however, were restless and unsubdued, and gave us much trouble, and it was these bands that necessitated the scouts.

My little son, Harry, four years old, was my constant and only companion, during that long, cold, and anxious winter.

My mother sent me an appealing invitation to come home for a year. I accepted gladly, and one afternoon in May, Jack put us aboard the Silver City stage, which passed daily through the post.

Our excellent Chinese servant promised to stay with the "Captain" and take care of him, and as I said "Goodbye, Hoo Chack," I noticed an expression of real regret on his usually stolid features.

Occupied with my thoughts, on entering the stage, I did not notice the passengers or the man sitting next me on the back seat. Darkness soon closed around us, and I suppose we fell asleep. Between naps, I heard a queer clanking sound, but supposed it was the chains of the harness or the stage-coach gear. The next morning, as we got out at a relay station for breakfast, I saw the handcuffs on the man next to whom I had sat all the night long. The sheriff was on the box outside. He very obligingly changed seats with me for the rest of the way, and evening found us on the overland train speeding on our journey East. Camp MacDermit with its dreary associations and surroundings faded gradually from my mind, like a dream.

The year of 1879 brought us several changes. My little daughter was born in mid-summer at our old home in Nantucket. As I lay watching the curtains move gently to and fro in the soft sea-breezes, and saw my mother and sister moving about the room, and a good old nurse rocking my baby in her arms, I could but think of those other days at Camp Apache, when I lay through the long hours, with my new-born baby by my side, watching, listening for someone to come in. There was no one, no woman to come, except the poor hard-working laundress of the cavalry, who did come once a day to care for the baby.

Ah! what a contrast! and I had to shut my eyes for fear I should cry, at the mere thought of those other days.

Jack took a year's leave of absence and joined me in the autumn at Nantucket, and the winter was spent in New York, enjoying the theatres and various amusements we had so long been deprived of. Here we met again Captain Porter and Carrie Wilkins, who was now Mrs. Porter. They were stationed at David's Island, one of the harbour posts, and we went over to see them. "Yes," he said, "as Jacob waited seven years for Rachel, so I waited for Carrie."

The following summer brought us the good news that Captain Corliss' company was ordered to Angel Island, in the bay of San Francisco. "Thank goodness," said Jack, "C company has got some good luck, at last!"

Joyfully we started back on the overland trip to California, which took about nine days at that time. Now, travelling with a year-old baby and a five-year-old boy was quite troublesome, and we were very glad when the train had crossed the bleak Sierras and swept down into the lovely valley of the Sacramento.

Arriving in San Francisco, we went to the old Occidental Hotel, and as we were going in to dinner, a card was handed to us. "Hoo Chack" was the name on the card. "That Chinaman!" I cried to Jack. "How do you suppose he knew we were here?"

We soon made arrangements for him to accompany us to Angel Island, and in a few days this "heathen Chinee" had unpacked all our boxes and made our quarters very comfortable. He was rather a high-caste man, and as true and loyal as a Christian. He never broke his word, and he staid with us as long as we remained in California.

And now we began to live, to truly live; for we felt that the years spent at those desert posts under the scorching suns of Arizona had cheated us out of all but a bare existence upon earth.

The flowers ran riot in our garden, fresh fruits and vegetables, fresh fish, and all the luxuries of that marvellous climate, were brought to our door.

A comfortable Government steamboat plied between San

Francisco and its harbour posts, and the distance was not great—only three quarters of an hour. So we had a taste of the social life of that fascinating city, and could enjoy the theatres also.

On the Island, we had music and dancing, as it was the headquarters of the regiment. Mrs. Kautz, so brilliant and gay, held grand court here—receptions, military functions, lawn tennis, bright uniforms, were the order of the day. And that incomparable climate! How I revelled in it! When the fog rolled in from the Golden Gate, and enveloped the great city of Saint Francis in its cold vapours, the Island of the Angels lay warm and bright in the sunshine.

The old Spaniards named it well, and the old Nantucket whalers who sailed around Cape Horn on their way to the Ar'tic, away back in the eighteen twenties, used to put in near there for water, and were well familiar with its bright shores, before it was touched by man's handiwork.

Was there ever such an emerald green as adorned those hills which sloped down to the bay? Could anything equal the fields of golden *escholzchia* which lay there in the sunshine? Or the blue masses of "baby-eye," which opened in the mornings and held up their pretty cups to catch the dew?

Was this a real Paradise?

It surely seemed so to us; and, as if Nature had not done enough, the Fates stepped in and sent all the agreeable young officers of the regiment there, to help us enjoy the heavenly spot.

There was Terrett, the handsome and aristocratic young Baltimorean, one of the finest men I ever saw in uniform; and Richardson, the stalwart Texan, and many others, with whom we danced and played tennis, and altogether there was so much to do and to enjoy that Time rushed by and we knew only that we were happy, and enchanted with Life.

Did any uniform ever equal that of the infantry in those days? The dark blue, heavily braided "blouse," the white stripe on the light blue trousers, the jaunty cap? And then, the straight backs and the slim lines of those youthful figures! It seems to me any woman who was not an Egyptian mummy would feel her heart thrill and her blood tingle at the sight of them.

Indians and deserts and Ehrenberg did not exist for me any-more. My girlhood seemed to have returned, and I enjoyed everything with the keenest zest.

My old friend Charley Bailey, who had married for his second wife a most accomplished young San Francisco girl, lived next door to us.

General and Mrs. Kautz entertained so hospitably, and were so beloved by all. Together Mrs. Kautz and I read the German classics, and went to the German theatre; and by and by a very celebrated player, Friedrich Haase, from the Royal Theatre of Berlin, came to San Francisco. We never missed a performance, and when his tour was over, Mrs. Kautz gave a lawn party at Angel Island for him and a few of the members of his company. It was charming. I well remember how the sun shone that day, and, as we strolled up from the boat with them, Frau Haase stopped, looked at the blue sky, the lovely clouds, the green slopes of the Island and said: *"Mein Gott! Frau Summerhayes, was ist das für ein Paradies! Warum haben Sie uns nicht gesagt, Sie wohnten im Paradies!"*

So, with music and German speech, and strolls to the North and to the South Batteries, that wonderful and never to-be-forgotten day with the great Friedrich Haase came to an end.

The months flew by, and the second winter found us still there; we heard rumours of Indian troubles in Arizona, and at last the orders came. The officers packed away their evening clothes in camphor and had their campaign clothes put out to air, and got their mess-chests in order, and the post was alive with preparations for the field. All the families were to stay behind. The most famous Indian renegade was to be hunted down, and serious fighting was looked for.

At last all was ready, and the day was fixed for the departure of the troops.

The winter rains had set in, and the skies were grey, as the command marched down to the boat.

The officers and soldiers were in their campaign clothes;

the latter had their blanket-rolls and haversacks slung over their shoulders, and their tin cups, which hung from the haversacks, rattled and jingled as they marched down in even columns of four, over the wet and grassy slopes of the parade ground, where so short a time before all had been glitter and sunshine.

I realized then perhaps for the first time what the uniform really stood for; that every man who wore it, was going out to fight—that they held their lives as nothing. The glitter was all gone; nothing but sad reality remained.

The officers' wives and the soldiers' wives followed the troops to the dock. The soldiers marched single file over the gang-plank of the boat, the officers said goodbye, the shrill whistle of the "General McPherson" sounded—and they were off. We leaned back against the coal-sheds, and soldiers' and officers' wives alike all wept together.

And now a season of gloom came upon us. The skies were dull and murky and the rain poured down.

Our old friend Bailey, who was left behind on account of illness, grew worse and finally his case was pronounced hopeless. His death added to the deep gloom and sadness which enveloped us all.

A few of the soldiers who had staid on the Island to take care of the post, carried poor Bailey to the boat, his casket wrapped in the flag and followed by a little procession of women. I thought I had never seen anything so sad.

The campaign lengthened out into months, but the California winters are never very long, and before the troops came back the hills looked their brightest green again. The campaign had ended with no very serious losses to our troops and all was joyous again, until another order took us from the sea-coast to the interior once more.

CHAPTER 29

Changing Station

It was the custom to change the stations of the different companies of a regiment about every two years. So the autumn of
'82 found us on the way to Fort Halleck, a post in Nevada, but
differing vastly from the desolate MacDermit station. Fort Halleck was only thirteen miles south of the Overland Railroad,
and lay near a spur of the Humboldt range. There were miles of
sage-brush between the railroad and the post, but the mountains
which rose abruptly five thousand feet on the far side, made
a magnificent background for the officers' quarters, which lay
nestled at the bottom of the foot-hills.

"Oh! what a lovely post!" I cried, as we drove in.

Major Sanford of the First Cavalry, with Captain Carr and
Lieutenant Oscar Brown, received us. "Dear me," I thought, "if
the First Cavalry is made up of such gallant men as these, the old
Eighth Infantry will have to look out for its laurels."

Mrs. Sanford and Mrs. Carr gave us a great welcome and vied
with each other in providing for our comfort, and we were soon
established.

It was so good to see the gay yellow of the cavalry again!
Now I rode, to my heart's content, and it was good to be alive;
to see the cavalry drill, and to ride through the canons, gorgeous
in their flaming autumn tints; then again to gallop through the
sage-brush, jumping where we could not turn, starting up rab-
bits by the score.

That little old post, now long since abandoned, marked a

pleasant epoch in our life. From the ranches scattered around we could procure butter and squabs and young vegetables, and the soldiers cultivated great garden patches, and our small dinners and breakfasts live in delightful memory.

At the end of two years spent so pleasantly with the people of the First Cavalry, our company was again ordered to Angel Island. But a second very active campaign in Arizona and Mexico, against Geronimo, took our soldiers away from us, and we passed through a period of considerable anxiety. June of '86 saw the entire regiment ordered to take station in Arizona once more.

We travelled to Tucson in a Pullman car. It was hot and uninteresting. I had been at Tucson nine years before, for a few hours, but the place seemed unfamiliar. I looked for the old tavern; I saw only the railroad restaurant. We went in to take breakfast, before driving out to the post of Fort Lowell, seven miles away. Everything seemed changed. Iced cantaloupe was served by a spick-span alert waiter; then, quail on toast. "Ice in Arizona?" It was like a dream, and I remarked to Jack, "This isn't the same Arizona we knew in '74," and then, "I don't believe I like it as well, either; all this luxury doesn't seem to belong to the place."

After a drive behind some smart mules, over a flat stretch of seven miles, we arrived at Fort Lowell, a rather attractive post, with a long line of officers' quarters, before which ran a level road shaded by beautiful great trees. We were assigned a half of one of these sets of quarters, and as our half had no conveniences for house-keeping, it was arranged that we should join a mess with General and Mrs. Kautz and their family. We soon got settled down to our life there, and we had various recreations; among them, driving over to Tucson and riding on horseback are those which I remember best.

We made a few acquaintances in Tucson, and they sometimes drove out in the evenings, or more frequently rode out on horseback. Then we would gather together on the Kautz *piazza* and everybody sang to the accompaniment of Mrs. Kautz's guitar. It was very hot, of course; we had all expected that, but the luxuries obtainable through the coming of the railroad, such as ice, and various summer drinks, and lemons, and butter, helped out to make the summer there more comfortable.

We slept on the *piazzas*, which ran around the houses on a level with the ground. At that time the fad for sleeping out of doors, at least amongst civilized people, did not exist, and our arrangements were entirely primitive.

Our quarters were surrounded by a small yard and a fence; the latter was dilapidated, and the gate swung on one hinge. We were seven miles from anywhere, and surrounded by a desolate country. I did not experience the feeling of terror that I had had at Camp Apache, for instance, nor the gruesome fear of the Ehrenberg grave-yard, nor the appalling fright I had known in crossing the Mogollon range or in driving through Sanford's Pass. But still there was a haunting feeling of insecurity which hung around me especially at night.

I was awfully afraid of snakes, and no sooner had we lain ourselves down on our cots to sleep, than I would hear a rustling among the dry leaves that had blown in under our beds. Then all would be still again; then a crackling and a rustling—in a flash I would be sitting up in bed. "Jack, do you hear that?"

Of course I did not dare to move or jump out of bed, so I would sit, rigid, scared. "Jack! what is it?"

"Nonsense, Mattie, go to sleep; it's the toads jumping about in the leaves." But my sleep was fitful and disturbed, and I never knew what a good night's rest was.

One night I was awakened by a tremendous snort right over my face. I opened my eyes and looked into the wild eyes of a big black bull. I think I must have screamed, for the bull ran clattering off the *piazza* and out through the gate. By this time Jack was up, and Harry and Katherine, who slept on the front *piazza*, came running out, and I said: "Well, this is the limit of all things, and if that gate isn't mended tomorrow, I will know the reason why."

Now I heard a vague rumour that there was a creature of this sort in or near the post, and that he had a habit of wandering around at night, but as I had never seen him, it had made no great impression on my mind. Jack had a great laugh at me, but I did not think then, nor do I now, that it was anything to be laughed at.

We had heard much of the old Mission of San Xavier del Bac, away the other side of Tucson. Mrs. Kautz decided to go over there and go into camp and paint a picture of San Xavier. It was about sixteen miles from Fort Lowell.

So all the camp paraphernalia was gotten ready and several of the officers joined the party, and we all went over to San Xavier and camped for a few days under the shadow of those beautiful old walls. This Mission is almost unknown to the American traveller.

Exquisite in colour, form and architecture, it stands there a silent reminder of the Past. The curious carvings and paintings inside the church, and the precious old vestments which were shown us by an ancient custodian, filled my mind with wonder. The building is partly in ruins, and the little squirrels were running about the galleries, but the great dome is intact, and many of the wonderful figures which ornament it.

Of course we know the Spanish built it about the middle or last of the sixteenth century, and that they tried to Christianize the tribes of Indians who lived around in the vicinity. But there is no sign of priest or communicant now, nothing but a desolate plain around it for miles. No one can possibly understand how the building of this large and beautiful mission was accomplished, and I believe history furnishes very little information. In its archives was found quite recently the charter given by Ferdinand and Isabella, to establish the *pueblo* of Tucson about the beginning of the 16th century.

After a few delightful days, we broke camp and returned to Fort Lowell.

And now the summer was drawing to a close, and we were anticipating the delights of the winter climate at Tucson, when, without a note of warning, came the orders for Fort Niobrara. We looked, appalled, in each other's faces, the evening the telegram came, for we did not even know where Fort Niobrara was.

We all rushed into Major Wilhelm's quarters, for he always knew everything. We (Mrs. Kautz and several of the other ladies of the post, and myself) were in a state of tremendous excitement. We pounded on Major Wilhelm's door and we heard a faint voice from his bedroom (for it was after ten o'clock); then we waited a few moments and he said, "Come in."

We opened the door, but there being no light in his quarters we could not see him. A voice said: "What in the name of—" but we did not wait for him to finish; we all shouted: "Where is Fort Niobrara?"

"The Devil!" he said. "Are we ordered there?"

"Yes, yes," we cried; "where is it?"

"Why, girls," he said, relapsing into his customary moderate tones, "It's a hell of a freezing cold place, away up north in Nebraska."

We turned our backs and went over to our quarters to have a consultation, and we all retired with sad hearts.

Now, just think of it! To come to Fort Lowell in July, only to move in November! What could it mean? It was hard to leave the sunny South, to spend the winter in those congealed regions in the North. We were but just settled, and now came another break-up!

Our establishment now, with two children, several servants, two saddle horses, and additional household furnishings, was not so simple as in the beginning of our army life, when three chests and a box or two contained our worldly goods. Each move we made was more difficult than the last; our allowance of baggage did not begin to cover what we had to take along, and this added greatly to the expense of moving.

The enormous waste attending a move, and the heavy outlay incurred in travelling and getting settled anew, kept us always poor; these considerations increased our chagrin over this unexpected change of station. There was nothing to be done, however. Orders are relentless, even if they seem senseless, which this one did, to the women, at least, of the Eighth Infantry.

CHAPTER 30

Fort Niobrara

The journey itself, however, was not to be dreaded, although it was so undesired. It was entirely by rail across New Mexico and Kansas, to St. Joseph, then up the Missouri River and then across the state to the westward. Finally, after four or five days, we reached the small frontier town of Valentine, in the very northwest corner of the bleak and desolate state of Nebraska. The post of Niobrara was four miles away, on the Niobrara (swift water) River.

Some officers of the Ninth Cavalry met us at the station with the post ambulances. There were six companies of our regiment, with headquarters and band.

It was November, and the drive across the rolling prairie-land gave us a fair glimpse of the country around. We crossed the old bridge over the Niobrara River, and entered the post. The snow lay already on the brown and barren hills, and the place struck a chill to my heart.

The Ninth Cavalry took care of all the officers' families until we could get established. Lieutenant Bingham, a handsome and distinguished-looking young bachelor, took us with our two children to his quarters, and made us delightfully at home. His quarters were luxuriously furnished, and he was altogether adorable. This, to be sure, helped to soften my first harsh impressions of the place.

Quarters were not very plentiful, and we were compelled to take a house occupied by a young officer of the Ninth. What base ingratitude it seemed, after the kindness we had accepted from his regiment! But there was no help for it. We secured a colored cook, who proved a very treasure, and on inquiring how she came to be in those wilds, I learned that she had accompanied a young heiress who eloped with a cavalry lieutenant, from her home in New York some years before.

What a contrast was here, and what a cruel contrast! With blood thinned down by the enervating summer at Tucson, here we were, thrust into the polar regions! Ice and snow and blizzards, blizzards and snow and ice! The mercury disappeared at the bottom of the thermometer, and we had nothing to mark any degrees lower than 40 below zero. Human calculations had evidently stopped there. Enormous box stoves were in every room and in the halls; the old-fashioned sort that we used to see in school-rooms and meeting-houses in New England. Into these, the soldiers stuffed great logs of mountain mahogany, and the fires were kept roaring day and night.

A board walk ran in front of the officers' quarters, and, desperate for fresh air and exercise, some of the ladies would bundle up and go to walk. But frozen chins, ears and elbows soon made this undesirable, and we gave up trying the fresh air, unless the mercury rose to 18 below, when a few of us would take our daily promenade.

We could not complain of our fare, however, for our larder hung full of all sorts of delicate and delicious things, brought in by the grangers, and which we were glad to buy. Prairie-chickens, young pigs, venison, and ducks, all hanging, to be used when desired.

To frappe a bottle of wine, we stood it on the porch; in a few minutes it would pour crystals. House-keeping was easy, but keeping warm was difficult.

It was about this time that the law was passed abolishing the post-trader's store, and forbidding the selling of whiskey to soldiers on a Government reservation. The pleasant canteen, or Post Exchange, the soldiers' club-room, was established, where the men could go to relieve the monotony of their lives.

With the abolition of whiskey, the tone of the post improved greatly; the men were contented with a glass of beer or light wine, the canteen was well managed, so the profits went back into the company messes in the shape of luxuries heretofore unknown; billiards and reading-rooms were established; and from that time on, the canteen came to be regarded in the army as a most excellent institution. The men gained in self-respect; the canteen provided them with a place where they could go and take a bite of lunch, read, chat, smoke, or play games with their own chosen friends, and escape the lonesomeness of the barracks.

But, alas! this condition of things was not destined to endure, for the women of the various Temperance societies, in their mistaken zeal and woeful ignorance of the soldiers' life, succeeded in influencing legislation to such an extent that the canteen, in its turn, was abolished; with what dire results, we of the army all know.

Those estimable women of the W. C. T. U. thought to do good to the army, no doubt, but through their pitiful ignorance of the soldiers' needs they have done him an incalculable harm.

Let them stay by their lectures and their clubs, I say, and their other amusements; let them exercise their good influences nearer home, with a class of people whose conditions are understood by them, where they can, no doubt, do worlds of good.

They cannot know the drear monotony of the barracks life on the frontier in times of peace. I have lived close by it, and I know it well. A ceaseless round of drill and work and lessons, and work and lessons and drill—no recreation, no excitement, no change.

Far away from family and all home companionship, a man longs for some pleasant place to go, after the day's work is done. Perhaps these women think (if, in their blind enthusiasm, they think at all) that a young soldier or an old soldier needs no recreation. At all events, they have taken from him the only one he had, the good old canteen, and given him nothing in return.

Now Fort Niobrara was a large post. There were ten companies, cavalry and infantry, General August V. Kautz, the Colonel of the Eighth Infantry, in command.

And here, amidst the sand-hills of Nebraska, we first began to really know our Colonel. A man of strong convictions and abiding honesty, a soldier who knew his profession thoroughly, having not only achieved distinction in the Civil War, but having served when little more than a boy, in the Mexican War of 1846. Genial in his manners, brave and kind, he was beloved by all.

The three Kautz children, Frankie, Austin, and Navarra, were the inseparable companions of our own children. There was a small school for the children of the post, and a soldier by the name of Delany was schoolmaster. He tried hard to make our children learn, but they did not wish to study, and spent all their spare time in planning tricks to be played upon poor Delany. It was a difficult situation for the soldier. Finally, the two oldest Kautz children were sent East to boarding-school, and we also began to realize that something must be done.

Our surroundings during the early winter, it is true, had been dreary enough, but as the weather softened a bit and the spring approached, the post began to wake up.

In the meantime, Cupid had not been idle. It was observed that Mr. Bingham, our gracious host of the Ninth Cavalry, had fallen in love with Antoinette, the pretty and attractive daughter of Captain Lynch of our own regiment, and the post began to be on the qui vive to see how the affair would end, for nobody expects to see the course of true love run smooth. In their case, however, the Fates were kind and in due time the happy engagement was announced.

We had an excellent amusement hall, with a fine floor for dancing. The chapel was at one end, and a fairly good stage was at the other.

Being nearer civilization now, in the state of Nebraska, Uncle Sam provided us with a chaplain, and a weekly service was held by the Anglican clergyman—a tall, well-formed man, a scholar and, as we say, a gentleman. He wore the uniform of the army chaplain, and as far as looks went could hold his own with any of the younger officers. And it was a great comfort to the church people to have this weekly service.

During the rest of the time, the chapel was concealed by heavy curtains, and the seats turned around facing the stage.

We had a good string orchestra of twenty or more pieces, and as there were a number of active young bachelors at the post, a series of weekly dances was inaugurated. Never did I enjoy dancing more than at this time.

Then Mrs. Kautz, who was a thorough music lover and had a cultivated taste as well as a trained and exquisite voice, gave several musicales, for which much preparation was made, and which were most delightful. These were given at the quarters of General Kautz, a long, low, rambling one-story house, arranged with that artistic taste for which Mrs. Kautz was distinguished.

Then came theatricals, all managed by Mrs. Kautz, whose talents were versatile.

We charged admission, for we needed some more scenery, and the neighbouring frontier town of Valentine came riding and driving over the prairie and across the old bridge of the Niobrara River, to see our plays. We had a well-lighted stage. Our methods were primitive, as there was no gas or electricity there in those days, but the results were good, and the histrionic ability shown by some of our young men and women seemed marvellous to us.

I remember especially Bob Emmet's acting, which moved me to tears, in a most pathetic love scene. I thought, "What has the stage lost, in this gifted man!"

But he is of a family whose talents are well known, and his personality, no doubt, added much to his natural ability as an actor.

Neither the army nor the stage can now claim this brilliant cavalry officer, as he was induced, by urgent family reasons, shortly after the period of which I am writing, to resign his commission and retire to private life, at the very height of his ambitious career.

And now the summer came on apace. A tennis-court was

made, and added greatly to our amusement. We were in the saddle every day, and the country around proved very attractive at this season, both for riding and driving.

But all this gayety did not content me, for the serious question of education for our children now presented itself; the question which, sooner or later, presents itself to the minds of all the parents of army children. It is settled differently by different people. It had taken a year for us to decide.

I made up my mind that the first thing to be done was to take the children East and then decide on schools afterwards. So our plans were completed and the day of departure fixed upon. Jack was to remain at the Post.

About an hour before I was to leave I saw the members of the string orchestra filing across the parade ground, coming directly towards our quarters. My heart began to beat faster, as I realized that Mrs. Kautz had planned a serenade for me. I felt it was a great break in my army life, but I did not know I was leaving the old regiment forever, the regiment with which I had been associated for so many years.

And as I listened to the beautiful strains of the music I loved so well, my eyes were wet with tears, and after all the goodbye's were said, to the officers and their wives, my friends who had shared all our joys and our sorrows in so many places and under so many conditions, I ran out to the stable and pressed my cheek against the soft warm noses of our two saddle horses. I felt that life was over for me, and nothing but work and care remained. I say I felt all this. It must have been premonition, for I had no idea that I was leaving the line of the army forever.

The ambulance was at the door, to take us to Valentine, where I bade Jack goodbye, and took the train for the East. His last promise was to visit us once a year, or whenever he could get a leave of absence.

My husband had now worn the single bar on his shoulder-strap for eleven years or more; before that, the straps of the second lieutenant had adorned his broad shoulders for a period quite as long. Twenty-two years a lieutenant in the regular army, after fighting, in a volunteer regiment of his own state, through the four years of the Civil War! The "gallant and meritorious service" for which he had received brevets, seemed, indeed, to have been forgotten. He had grown grey in Indian campaigns, and it looked as if the frontier might always be the home of the senior lieutenant of the old Eighth. Promotion in that regiment had been at a standstill for years.

Being in Washington for a short time towards mid-winter enjoying the social side of military life at the Capital, an opportunity came to me to meet President Cleveland, and although his administration was nearing its close, and the stress of official cares was very great, he seemed to have leisure and interest to ask me about my life on the frontier; and as the conversation became quite personal, the impulse seized me, to tell him just how I felt about the education of our children, and then to tell him what I thought and what others thought about the unjust way in which the promotions and retirements in our regiment had been managed.

He listened with the greatest interest and seemed pleased with my frankness. He asked me what the soldiers and officers out there thought of "So and So."

"They hate him," I said.

Whereupon he laughed outright and I knew I had committed an indiscretion, but life on the frontier does not teach one diplomacy of speech, and by that time I was nerved up to say just what I felt, regardless of results.

"Well," he said, smiling, "I am afraid I cannot interfere much with those military matters;" then, pointing with his left hand and thumb towards the War Department, "they fix them all up over there in the Adjutant General's office," he added.

Then he asked me many more questions; if I had always stayed out there with my husband, and why I did not live in the East, as so many army women did; and all the time I could hear the dull thud of the carpenters' hammers, for they were building even then the board seats for the public who would witness the inaugural ceremonies of his successor, and with each stroke of the hammer, his face seemed to grow more sad.

I felt the greatness of the man; his desire to be just and good: his marvellous personal power, his ability to understand and to sympathize, and when I parted from him he said again laughingly, "Well, I shall not forget your husband's regiment, and if anything turns up for those fine men you have told me about, they will hear from me." And I knew they were the words of a man, who meant what he said.

In the course of our conversation he had asked, "Who are these men? Do they ever come to Washington? I rarely have these things explained to me and I have little time to interfere with the decisions of the Adjutant General's office."

I replied: "No, Mr. President, they are not the men you see around Washington. Our regiment stays on the frontier, and these men are the ones who do the fighting, and you people here in Washington are apt to forget all about them."

"What have they ever done? Were they in the Civil War?" he asked.

"Their records stand in black and white in the War Department," I replied, "if you have the interest to learn more about them."

"Women's opinions are influenced by their feelings," he said.

"Mine are based upon what I know, and I am prepared to stand by my convictions," I replied.

Soon after this interview, I returned to New York and I did not give the matter very much further thought, but my impression of the greatness of Mr. Cleveland and of his powerful personality has remained with me to this day.

A vacancy occurred about this time in the Quartermaster's Department, and the appointment was eagerly sought for by many lieutenants of the army. President Cleveland saw fit to give the appointment to Lieutenant Summerhayes, making him a captain and quartermaster, and then, another vacancy occurring shortly after, he appointed Lieutenant John McEwen Hyde to be also a captain and quartermaster.

Lieutenant Hyde stood next in rank to my husband and had

grown grey in the old Eighth Infantry. So the regiment came in for its honour at last, and General Kautz, when the news of the second appointment reached him, exclaimed, "Well! well! does the President think my regiment a nursery for the Staff?"

The Eighth Foot and the Ninth Horse at Niobrara gave the new captain and quartermaster a rousing farewell, for now my husband was leaving his old regiment forever; and, while he appreciated fully the honour of his new staff position, he felt a sadness at breaking off the associations of so many years—a sadness which can scarcely be understood by the young officers of the present day, who are promoted from one regiment to another, and rarely remain long enough with one organization to know even the men of their own Company.

There were many champagne suppers, dinners and card-parties given for him, to make the goodbye something to be remembered, and at the end of a week's festivities, he departed by a night train from Valentine, thus eluding the hospitality of those generous but wild frontiersmen, who were waiting to give him what they call out there a "send-off."

For Valentine was like all frontier towns; a row of stores and saloons. The men who kept them were generous, if somewhat rough. One of the officers of the post, having occasion to go to the railroad station one day at Valentine, saw the body of a man hanging to a telegraph pole a short distance up the track. He said to the station man: "What does that mean?" (nodding his head in the direction of the telegraph pole).

"Why, it means just this," said the station man, "the people who hung that man last night had the nerve to put him right in front of this place, by G—. What would the passengers think of this town, sir, as they went by? Why, the reputation of Valentine would be ruined! Yes, sir, we cut him down and moved him up a pole or two. He was a hard case, though," he added.

CHAPTER 31

Santa Fe

I made haste to present Captain Summerhayes with the shoulder-straps of his new rank, when he joined me in New York.

The orders for Santa Fe reached us in mid-summer at Nantucket. I knew about as much of Santa Fe as the average American knows, and that was nothing; but I did know that the Staff appointment solved the problem of education for us (for Staff officers are usually stationed in cities), and I knew that our frontier life was over. I welcomed the change, for our children were getting older, and we were ourselves approaching the age when comfort means more to one than it heretofore has.

Jack obeyed his sudden orders, and I followed him as soon as possible.

Arriving at Santa Fe in the mellow sunlight of an October day, we were met by my husband and an officer of the Tenth Infantry, and as we drove into the town, its appearance of placid content, its ancient buildings, its great trees, its clear air, its friendly, indolent-looking inhabitants, gave me a delightful feeling of home. A mysterious charm seemed to possess me. It was the spell which that old town loves to throw over the strangers who venture off the beaten track to come within her walls.

Lying only eighteen miles away, over a small branch road from Llamy (a station on the Atchison and Topeka Railroad), few people take the trouble to stop over to visit it. "Dead old town," says the commercial traveller, "nothing doing there."

And it is true.

But no spot that I have visited in this country has thrown around me the spell of enchantment which held me fast in that sleepy and historic town.

The Governor's Palace, the old *plaza*, the ancient churches, the antiquated customs, the Sisters' Hospital, the old Convent of Our Lady of Loretto, the soft music of the Spanish tongue, I loved them all.

There were no factories; no noise was ever heard; the sun shone peacefully on, through winter and summer alike. There was no cold, no heat, but a delightful year-around climate. Why the place was not crowded with health seekers, was a puzzle to me. I had thought that the bay of San Francisco offered the most agreeable climate in America, but, in the Territory of New Mexico, Santa Fe was the perfection of all climates combined.

The old city lies in the broad valley of the Santa Fe Creek, but the valley of the Santa Fe Creek lies seven thousand feet above the sea level. I should never have known that we were living at a great altitude, if I had not been told, for the equable climate made us forget to inquire about height or depth or distance.

I listened to old Father de Fourri preach his short sermons in English to the few Americans who sat on one side of the aisle, in the church of Our Lady of Guadaloupe; then, turning with an easy gesture towards his Mexican congregation, who sat or knelt near the sanctuary, and saying, "*Hermanos mios,*" he gave the same discourse in good Spanish. I felt comfortable in the thought that I was improving my Spanish as well as profiting by Father de Fourri's sound logic. This good priest had grown old at Santa Fe in the service of his church.

The Mexican women, with their black *ribosos* wound around their heads and concealing their faces, knelt during the entire mass, and made many long responses in Latin.

After years spent in a heathenish manner, as regards all church observations, this devout and unique service, following the customs of ancient Spain, was interesting to me in the extreme.

Sometimes on a Sunday afternoon I attended Vespers in the

chapel of the Sisters' Hospital (as it was called). A fine *Sanitarium*, managed entirely by the Roman Catholic Sisters of Charity.

Sister Victoria, who was at the head of the management, was not only a very beautiful woman, but she had an agreeable voice and always led in the singing.

It seemed like Heaven.

I wrote to my friends in the East to come to the Sisters' Hospital if they wanted health, peace and happiness, for it was surely to be found there. I visited the convent of Our Lady of Loretto: I stood before a high wall in an embrasure of which there was a low wooden gate; I pulled on a small knotted string which hung out of a little hole, and a queer old bell rang. Then one of the nuns came and let me in, across a beautiful garden to the convent school. I placed my little daughter as a day pupil there, as she was now eleven years old. The nuns spoke very little English and the children none at all.

The entire city was ancient, Spanish, Catholic, steeped in a religious atmosphere and in what the average American Protestant would call the superstitions of the dark ages. There were endless fiestas, and processions and religious services, I saw them all and became much interested in reading the history of the Catholic missions, established so early out through what was then a wild and unexplored country. After that, I listened with renewed interest to old Father de Fouri, who had tended and led his flock of simple people so long and so lovingly.

There was a large painting of Our Lady of Guadaloupe over the altar—these people firmly believed that she had appeared to them, on the earth, and so strong was the influence around me that I began almost to believe it too. I never missed the Sunday morning mass, and I fell in easily with the religious observances.

I read and studied about the old explorers, and I seemed to live in the time of Cortez and his brave band. I became acquainted with Adolf Bandelier, who had lived for years in that country, engaged in research for the American Archaeological Society. I visited the Indian *pueblos*, those marvellous structures of *adobe*, where live entire tribes, and saw natives who have not changed their manner of speech or dress since the days when the Spaniards first penetrated to their curious dwellings, three hundred or more years ago. I climbed the rickety ladders, by which one enters these strange dwellings, and bought the great bowls which these Indians shape in some manner without the assistance of a potter's wheel, and then bake in their mud ovens.

The *pueblo* of Tesuque is only nine miles from Santa Fe, and a pleasant drive, at that; it seemed strange to me that the road was not lined with tourists. But no, they pass all these wonders by, in their disinclination to go off the beaten track.

Visiting the *pueblos* gets to be a craze. Governor and Mrs. Prince knew them all—the *pueblo* of Taos, of Santa Clara, San Juan, and others; and the Governor's collection of great stone idols was a marvel indeed. He kept them laid out on shelves, which resembled the bunks on a great vessel, and in an apartment especially reserved for them, in his residence at Santa Fe, and it was always with considerable awe that I entered that apartment. The Governor occupied at that time a low, rambling *adobe* house, on Palace Avenue, and this, with its thick walls and low window-seats, made a fit setting for the treasures they had gathered.

Later on, the Governor's family occupied the palace (as it is always called) of the old Spanish Viceroy, a most ancient, picturesque, yet dignified building, facing the *plaza*.

The various apartments in this old palace were used for Government offices when we were stationed there in 1889, and in one of these rooms, General Lew Wallace, a few years before, had written his famous book, *Ben Hur*.

On the walls were hanging old portraits painted by the Spaniards in the sixteenth century. They were done on rawhide, and whether these interesting and historic pictures have been preserved by our Government I do not know.

The distinguished Anglican clergyman living there taught a small class of boys, and the "Academy," an excellent school established by the Presbyterian Board of Missions, afforded good advantages for the young girls of the garrison. And as we had found that the Convent of Loretto was not just adapted to the education of an American child, we withdrew Katharine from that school and placed her at the Presbyterian Academy.

To be sure, the young woman teacher gave a rousing lecture on total abstinence once a week; going even so far as to say, that to partake of apple sauce which had begun to ferment was yielding to the temptations of Satan. The young woman's arguments made a disastrous impression upon our children's minds; so much so, that the rich German Jews whose daughters attended the school complained greatly; for, as they told us, these girls would hasten to snatch the decanters from the sideboard, at the approach of visitors, and hide them, and they began to sit in judgment upon their elders.

Now these men were among the leading citizens of the town; they were self-respecting and wealthy. They could not stand these extreme doctrines, so opposed to their life and their traditions. We informed Miss X. one day that she could excuse our children from the total abstinence lecture, or we should be compelled to withdraw them from the school. She said she could not compel them to listen, but preach she must. She remained obedient to her orders from the Board, and we could but respect her for that. Our young daughters were, however, excused from the lecture.

But our time was not entirely given up to the study of ancient pottery, for the social life there was delightful. The garrison was in the centre of the town, the houses were comfortable, and the streets shaded by old trees. The Tenth Infantry had its headquarters and two companies there. Every afternoon, the military band played in the *Plaza*, where everybody went and sat on benches in the shade of the old trees, or, if cool, in the delightful sunshine. The pretty and well-dressed *senoritas* cast shy glances at the young officers of the Tenth; but, alas! the handsome and attractive Lieutenants Van Vliet and Seyburn, and the more sedate Lieutenant Plummer, could not return these bewitching glances, as they were all settled in life.

The two former officers had married in Detroit, and both Mrs. Van Vliet and Mrs. Seyburn did honour to the beautiful city of Michigan, for they were most agreeable and clever women, and presided over their army homes with distinguished grace and hospitality.

The Americans who lived there were all professional people; mostly lawyers, and a few bankers. I could not understand why so many Eastern lawyers lived there. I afterwards learned that the old Spanish land grants had given rise to illimitable and never-ending litigation.

Every morning we rode across country. There were no fences, but the wide irrigation ditches gave us a plenty of excitement, and the riding was glorious. I had no occasion yet to realize that we had left the line of the army.

A camping trip to the head-waters of the Pecos, where we caught speckled trout in great abundance in the foaming riffles and shallow pools of this rushing mountain stream, remaining in camp a week under the spreading boughs of the mighty pines, added to the variety and delights of our life there.

With such an existence as this, good health and diversion, the time passed rapidly by.

It was against the law now for soldiers to marry; the old days of "laundresses" had passed away. But the trombone player of the Tenth Infantry band (a young Boston boy) had married a wife, and now a baby had come to them. They could get no quarters, so we took the family in, and, as the wife was an excellent cook, we were able to give many small dinners. The walls of the house being three feet thick, we were never troubled by the trombone practice or the infant's cries. And many a delightful evening we had around the board, with Father de Fourri, Rev. Mr. Meany (the Anglican clergyman), the officers and ladies of the Tenth, Governor and Mrs. Prince, and the brilliant lawyer folk of Santa Fe.

Such an ideal life cannot last long; this existence of ours does not seem to be contrived on those lines. At the end of a year, orders came for Texas, and perhaps it was well that orders came, or we might be in Santa Fe today, wrapt in a dream of past ages; for the city of the Holy Faith had bound us with invisible chains.

With our departure from Santa Fe, all picturesqueness came to an end in our army life. Ever after that, we had really good houses to live in, which had all modern arrangements; we had beautiful, well-kept lawns and gardens, the same sort of domestic service that civilians have, and lived almost the same life.

CHAPTER 32

Texas

Whenever I think of San Antonio and Fort Sam Houston, the perfume of the wood violet which blossomed in mid-winter along the borders of our lawn, and the delicate odour of the Cape jessamine, seem to be wafted about me.

Fort Sam Houston is the Headquarters of the Department of Texas, and all the Staff officers live there, in comfortable stone houses, with broad lawns shaded by chinaberry trees. Then at the top of the hill is a great quadrangle, with a clock tower and all the department offices. On the other side of this quadrangle is the post, where the line officers live.

General Stanley commanded the Department. A fine, dignified and able man, with a great record as an Indian fighter. Jack knew him well, as he had been with him in the first preliminary survey for the northern Pacific Railroad, when he drove old Sitting Bull back to the Powder River.

He was now about to reach the age of retirement; and as the day approached, that day when a man has reached the limit of his usefulness (in the opinion of an ever-wise Government), that day which sounds the knell of active service, that day so dreaded and yet so longed for, that day when an army officer is sixty-four years old and Uncle Sam lays him upon the shelf, as that day approached, the city of San Antonio, in fact the entire State of Texas poured forth to bid him Godspeed; for if ever an army man was beloved, it was General Stanley by the State of Texas.

Now on the other side of the great quadrangle lay the post,

where were the soldiers' barracks and quarters of the line officers. This was commanded by Colonel Coppinger, a gallant officer, who had fought in many wars in many countries.

He had his famous regiment, the Twenty-third Infantry, and many were the pleasant dances and theatricals we had, with the music furnished by their band; for, as it was a time of peace, the troops were all in garrison.

Major Burbank was there also, with his well-drilled Light Battery of the 3rd Artillery.

My husband, being a captain and quartermaster, served directly under General George H. Weeks, who was Chief Quartermaster of the Department, and I can never forget his kindness to us both. He was one of the best men I ever knew, in the army or out of it, and came to be one of my dearest friends. He possessed the sturdy qualities of his Puritan ancestry, united with the charming manners of an aristocrat.

We belonged, of course, now, with the Staff, and something, an intangible something, seemed to have gone out of the life. The officers were all older, and the Staff uniforms were more sombre. I missed the white stripe of the infantry, and the yellow of the cavalry. The shoulder-straps all had gold eagles or leaves on them, instead of the Captains' or Lieutenants' bars. Many of the Staff officers wore civilians' clothes, which distressed me much, and I used to tell them that if I were Secretary of War they would not be permitted to go about in black alpaca coats and cinnamon-brown trousers.

"What would you have us do?" said General Weeks.

"Wear white duck and brass buttons," I replied.

"Fol-de-rol!" said the fine-looking and erect chief quartermaster; "you would have us be as vain as we were when we were Lieutenants?"

"You can afford to be," I answered; for, even with his threescore years, he had retained the lines of youth, and was, in my opinion, the finest looking man in the Staff of the Army.

But all my reproaches and all my diplomacy were of no avail in reforming the Staff. Evidently comfort and not looks was their motto.

One day, I accidentally caught a side view of myself in a long mirror (long mirrors had not been very plentiful on the frontier), and was appalled by the fact that my own lines corresponded but too well, alas! with those of the Staff. Ah, me! were the days, then, of Lieutenants forever past and gone? The days of suppleness and youth, the careless gay days, when there was no thought for the future, no anxiety about education, when the day began with a wild dash across country and ended with a dinner and dance—were they over, then, for us all?

Major Burbank's battery of light artillery came over and enlivened the quiet of our post occasionally with their brilliant red colour. At those times, we all went out and stood in the music pavilion to watch the drill; and when his horses and guns and caissons thundered down the hill and swept by us at a terrific gallop, our hearts stood still. Even the dignified Staff permitted themselves a thrill, and as for us women, our excitement knew no bounds.

The brilliant red of the artillery brought colour to the rather grey aspect of the quiet Headquarters post, and the magnificent drill supplied the martial element so dear to a woman's heart.

In San Antonio, the New has almost obliterated the Old, and little remains except its pretty green river, its picturesque bridges, and the historic Alamo, to mark it from other cities in the Southwest.

In the late afternoon, everybody drove to the *Plaza*, where all the country people were selling their garden-stuff and poultry in the open square. This was charming, and we all bought live fowl and drove home again. One heard cackling and gobbling from the smart traps and victorias, and it seemed to be a survival of an old custom. The whole town took a drive after that, and supped at eight o'clock.

The San Antonio people believe there is no climate to equal theirs, and talk much about the cool breezes from the Gulf of Mexico, which is some miles away. But I found seven months of the twelve too hot for comfort, and I could never detect much coolness in the summer breezes.

After I settled down to the sedateness which is supposed to belong to the Staff, I began to enjoy life very much. There is compensation for every loss, and I found, with the new friends, many of whom had lived their lives, and had known sorrow and joy, a true companionship which enriched my life, and filled the days with gladness.

My son had completed the High School course in San Antonio, under an able German master, and had been sent East to prepare for the Stevens Institute of Technology, and in the following spring I took my daughter Katharine and fled from the dreaded heat of a Texas summer. Never can I forget the child's grief on parting from her Texas pony. She extorted a solemn promise from her father, who was obliged to stay in Texas, that he would never part with him.

My brother, then unmarried, and my sister Harriet were living together in New Rochelle and to them we went. Harry's vacation enabled him to be with us, and we had a delightful summer. It was good to be on the shores of Long Island Sound.

In the autumn, not knowing what next was in store for us, I placed my dear little Katharine at the Convent of the Sacred Heart at Kenwood on the Hudson, that she might be able to complete her education in one place, and in the care of those lovely, gentle and refined ladies of that order.

Shortly after that, Captain Jack was ordered to David's Island, New York Harbor (now called Fort Slocum), where we spent four happy and uninterrupted years, in the most constant intercourse with my dear brother and sister.

Old friends were coming and going all the time, and it seemed so good to us to be living in a place where this was possible.

Captain Summerhayes was constructing officer and had a busy life, with all the various sorts of building to be done there.

David's Island was then an Artillery Post, and there were several batteries stationed there. (Afterwards it became a recruiting station.) The garrison was often entirely changed. At one time, General Henry C. Cook was in command. He and his charming Southern wife added so much to the enjoyment of the post. Then came our old friends the Van Vliets of Santa Fe days; and Dr. and Mrs. Valery Havard, who are so well known in the army, and then Colonel Carl Woodruff and Mrs. Woodruff, whom we all liked so much, and dear Doctor Julian Cabell, and others, who completed a delightful garrison.

And we had a series of informal dances and invited the distinguished members of the artist colony from New Rochelle, and it was at one of these dances that I first met Frederic Remington. I had long admired his work and had been most anxious to meet him. As a rule, Frederic did not attend any social functions, but he loved the army, and as Mrs. Remington was fond of social life, they were both present at our first little invitation dance.

About the middle of the evening I noticed Mr. Remington sitting alone and I crossed the hall and sat down beside him. I then told him how much I had loved his work and how it appealed to all army folks, and how glad I was to know him, and I suppose I said many other things such as literary men and painters and players often have to hear from enthusiastic women like myself. However, Frederic seemed pleased, and made some modest little speech and then fell into an abstracted silence, gazing on the great flag which was stretched across the hall at one end, and from behind which some few soldiers who were going to assist in serving the supper were passing in and out. I fell in with his mood immediately, as he was a person with whom formality was impossible, and said: "What are you looking at, Mr. Remington?"

He replied, turning upon me his round boyish face and his blue eyes gladdening, "I was just thinking I wished I was behind in there where those blue jackets are—you know—behind that flag with the soldiers—those are the men I like to study, you know, I don't like all this fuss and feathers of society"—then, blushing at his lack of gallantry, he added: "It's all right, of course, pretty women and all that, and I suppose you think I'm dreadful and—do you want me to dance with you—that's the proper thing here isn't it?"Whereupon, he seized me in his great arms and whirled me around at a pace I never dreamed of, and, once around, he said, "that's enough of this thing, isn't it, let's sit down, I believe I'm going to like you, though I'm not much for women."

I said "You must come over here often;" and he replied, "You've got a lot of jolly good fellows over here and I will do it."

Afterwards, the Remingtons and ourselves became the closest friends. Mrs. Remington's maiden name was Eva Caton, and after the first few meetings, she became "little Eva" to me—and if ever there was an embodiment of that gentle lovely name and what it implies, it is this woman, the wife of the great artist, who has stood by him through all the reverses of his early life and been, in every sense, his guiding star.

And now began visits to the studio, a great room he had built on to his house at New Rochelle. It had an enormous fire place where great logs were burned, and the walls were hung with the most rare and wonderful Indian curios. There he did all the painting which has made him famous in the last twenty years, and all the modelling which has already become so well known and would have eventually made him a name as a great sculptor. He always worked steadily until three o'clock and then there was a walk or game of tennis or a ride. After dinner, delightful evenings in the studio.

Frederic was a student and a deep thinker. He liked to solve all questions for himself and did not accept readily other men's theories. He thought much on religious subjects and the future life, and liked to compare the Christian religion with the religions of Eastern countries, weighing them one against the other with fairness and clear logic.

And so we sat, many evenings into the night, Frederic and Jack stretched in their big leather chairs puffing away at their pipes, Eva with her needlework, and myself a rapt listener: wondering at this man of genius, who could work with his creative brush all day long and talk with the eloquence of a learned

Doctor of Divinity half the night.

During the time we were stationed at Davids Island, Mr. Remington and Jack made a trip to the Southwest, where they shot the peccary (wild hog) in Texas and afterwards blue quail and other game in Mexico. Artist and soldier, they got on famously together notwithstanding the difference in their ages.

And now he was going to try his hand at a novel, a real romance. We talked a good deal about the little Indian boy, and I got to love White Weasel long before he appeared in print as John Ermine. The book came out after we had left New Rochelle—but I received a copy from him, and wrote him my opinion of it, which was one of unstinted praise. But it did not surprise me to learn that he did not consider it a success from a financial point of view.

"You see," he said a year afterwards, "that sort of thing does not interest the public. What they want,"—here he began to mimic some funny old East Side person, and both hands gesticulating—"is a backyard and a cabbage patch and a cook stove and babies' clothes drying beside it, you see, Mattie," he said. "They don't want to know anything about the Indian or the half-breed, or what he thinks or believes." And then he went off into one of his irresistible tirades combining ridicule and abuse of the reading public, in language such as only Frederic Remington could use before women and still retain his dignity.

"Well, Frederic," I said, "I will try to recollect that, when I write my experiences of Army Life."

In writing him my opinion of his book the year before, I had said, "In fact, I am in love with John Ermine." The following Christmas he sent me the accompanying card.

Now the book was dramatized and produced, with Hackett as John Ermine, at the Globe Theatre in September of 1902—the hottest weather ever on record in Boston at that season. Of course seats were reserved for us; we were living at Nantucket that year, and we set sail at noon to see the great production. We snatched a bite of supper at a nearby hotel in Boston and hurried to the theatre, but being late, had some difficulty in getting our seats. The curtain was up and there sat Hackett, not with long yellow hair (which was the salient point in the half-breed scout) but rather well-groomed, looking more like a parlour Indian than a real live half-breed, such as all we army people knew. I thought "this will never do."

The house was full, Hackett did the part well, and the audience murmured on going out: "a very artistic success." But the play was too mystical, too sad. It would have suited the "New Theatre" patrons better. I wrote him from Nantucket and criticized one or two minor points, such as the 1850 riding habits of the women, which were slouchy and unbecoming and made the army people look like poor emigrants and I received this letter in reply:

Webster Avenue, New Rochelle, N.Y.

My dear Mrs. S.,

Much obliged for your talk—it is just what we want-proper impressions.

I fought for that long hair but the management said the audience has got to, have some Hackett—why I could not see—but he is a matinee idol and that long with the box office.

We'll dress Katherine up better.

The long rehearsals at night nearly killed me—I was completely done up and came home on train Monday in that terrific heat and now I am in the hands of a doctor. Imagine me a week without sleep.

Hope that fight took Jack back to his youth. For the stage I don't think it was bad. We'll get grey shirts on their men later.

The old lady arrives today—she has been in Gloversville.

I think the play will go—but, we may have to save Ermine. The public is a funny old cat and won't stand for the mustard.

Well, glad you had a good time and of course you can't charge me up with the heat.

Yours, Frederick R.

Remington made a trip to the Yellowstone Park and this is what he wrote to Jack. His letters were never dated.

My dear Summerhayes:
Say if you could get a few puffs of this cold air out here you would think you were full of champagne water. I feel like a d— kid—
I thought I should never be young again—but here I am only 14 years old—my whiskers are falling out.
Capt. Brown of the 1st Cav. wishes to be remembered to you both. He is Park Superintendent. Says if you will come out here he will take care of you and he would.
Am painting and doing some good work. Made a "govt. six" yesterday.

In the course of time, he bought an island in the St. Lawrence and they spent several summers there.

On the occasion of my husband accepting a detail in active service in Washington at the Soldiers' Home, after his retirement, he received the following letter.

Ingleneuk, Chippewa Bay, N.Y.
My dear Jack—
So there you are—and I'm d— glad you are so nicely fixed. It's the least they could do for you and you ought to be able to enjoy it for ten years before they find any spavins on you if you will behave yourself, but I guess you will drift into that Army and Navy Club and round up with a lot of those old alkalied prairie-dogs whom neither Indians nor whiskey could kill and Mr. Gout will take you over his route to Arlington.
I'm on the water wagon and I feel like a young mule. I am never going to get down again to try the walking. If I lose my whip I am going to drive right on and leave it.
We are having a fine summer and I may run over to Washington this winter and throw my eye over you to see how you go. We made a trip down to New Foundland but saw nothing worthwhile. I guess I am getting to be an old

swat—I can't see anything that didn't happen twenty years ago,

Y— Frederick R.

At the close of the year just gone, this great soul passed from the earth leaving a blank in our lives that nothing can ever fill. Passed into the great Beyond whose mysteries were always troubling his mind. Suddenly and swiftly the call came—the hand was stilled and the restless spirit took its flight.

CHAPTER 33

David's Island

At Davids' Island the four happiest years of my army life glided swiftly away.

There was a small steam tug which made regular and frequent trips over to New Rochelle and we enjoyed our intercourse with the artists and players who lived there.

Zogbaum, whose well known pictures of sailors and warships and soldiers had reached us even in the far West, and whose charming family added so much to our pleasure.

Julian Hawthorne with his daughter Hildegarde, now so well known as a literary critic; Henry Loomis Nelson, whose fair daughter Margaret came to our little dances and promptly fell in love with a young, slim, straight Artillery officer. A case of love at first sight, followed by a short courtship and a beautiful little country wedding at Miss Nelson's home on the old Pelham Road, where Hildegarde Hawthorne was bridesmaid in a white dress and scarlet flowers (the artillery colours) and many famous literary people from everywhere were present.

Augustus Thomas, the brilliant playwright, whose home was near the Remingtons on Lathers' Hill, and whose wife, so young, so beautiful and so accomplished, made that home attractive and charming.

Francis Wilson, known to the world at large, first as a singer in comic opera, and now as an actor and author, also lived in New Rochelle, and we came to have the honour of being numbered amongst his friends. A devoted husband and kind father, a man of letters and a book lover, such is the man as we knew him in his home and with his family.

And now came the delicious warm summer days. We persuaded the quartermaster to prop up the little row of old bathing houses which had toppled over with the heavy winter gales. There were several bathing enthusiasts amongst us; we had a pretty fair little stretch of beach which was set apart for the officers' families, and now what bathing parties we had! Kemble, the illustrator, joined our ranks—and on a warm summer morning the little old Tug Hamilton was gay with the artists and their families, the players and writers of plays, and soon you could see the little garrison hastening to the beach and the swimmers running down the long pier, down the runway and off head first into the clear waters of the Sound.

What a company was that! The younger and the older ones all together, children and their fathers and mothers, all happy, all well, all so gay, and we of the frontier so enamoured of civilization and what it brought us! There were no intruders and ah! those were happy days. Uncle Sam seemed to be making up to us for what we had lost during all those long years in the wild places.

Then Augustus Thomas wrote the play of *Arizona* and we went to New York to see it put on, and we sat in Mr. Thomas' box and saw our frontier life brought before us with startling reality.

And so one season followed another. Each bringing its pleasures, and then came another lovely wedding, for my brother Harry gave up his bachelor estate and married one of the nicest and handsomest girls in Westchester County, and their home in New Rochelle was most attractive. My son was at the Stevens Institute and both he and Katharine were able to spend their vacations at David's Island, and altogether, our life there was near to perfection.

We were doomed to have one more tour in the West, however, and this time it was the Middle West.

For in the autumn of '96, Jack was ordered to Jefferson Barracks, Missouri, on construction work.

Jefferson Barracks is an old and historic post on the Mississippi River, some ten miles south of St. Louis. I could not seem to take any interest in the post or in the life there. I could not form new ties so quickly, after our life on the coast, and I did not like the Mississippi Valley, and St. Louis was too far from the post, and the trolley ride over there too disagreeable for words. After seven months of just existing (on my part) at Jefferson Barracks, Jack received an order for Fort Myer, the end, the aim, the dream of all army people. Fort Myer is about three miles from Washington, D. C.

We lost no time in getting there and were soon settled in our pleasant quarters. There was some building to be done, but the duty was comparatively light, and we entered with considerable zest into the social life of the Capital. We expected to remain there for two years, at the end of which time Captain Summerhayes would be retired and Washington would be our permanent home.

But alas! our anticipation was never to be realized, for, as we all know, in May of 1898, the Spanish War broke out, and my husband was ordered to New York City to take charge of the Army Transport Service, under Colonel Kimball.

No delay was permitted to him, so I was left behind, to pack up the household goods and to dispose of our horses and carriages as best I could.

The battle of Manila Bay had changed the current of our lives, and we were once more adrift.

The young cavalry officers came in to say goodbye to Captain Jack: everyone was busy packing up his belongings for an indefinite period and preparing for the field. We all felt the undercurrent of sadness and uncertainty, but "a good health" and "happy return" was drunk all around, and Jack departed at midnight for his new station and new duties.

The next morning at daybreak we were awakened by the tramp, tramp of the cavalry, marching out of the post, *en route* for Cuba.

We peered out of the windows and watched the troops we loved so well, until every man and horse had vanished from our sight.

Fort Myer was deserted and our hearts were sad.

My sister Harriet, who was visiting us at that time, returned from her morning walk, and as she stepped upon the porch, she said: "Well! of all lonesome places I ever saw, this is the worst yet. I am going to pack my trunk and leave. I came to visit an army post, but not an old women's home or an orphan asylum: that is about all this place is now. I simply cannot stay!"

Whereupon, she proceeded immediately to carry out her resolution, and I was left behind with my young daughter, to finish and close up our life at Fort Myer.

To describe the year which followed, that strenuous year in New York, is beyond my power.

That summer gave Jack his promotion to a major, but the anxiety and the terrible strain of official work broke down his health entirely, and in the following winter the doctors sent him to Florida, to recuperate.

After six weeks in St. Augustine, we returned to New York. The stress of the war was over; the major was ordered to Governor's Island as Chief Quartermaster, Department of the East, and in the following year he was retired, by operation of the law, at the age limit.

I was glad to rest from the incessant changing of stations; the life had become irksome to me, in its perpetual unrest. I was glad to find a place to lay my head, and to feel that we were not under orders; to find and to keep a roof-tree, under which we could abide forever.

In 1903, by an act of Congress, the veterans of the Civil War, who had served continuously for thirty years or more were given an extra grade, so now my hero wears with complacency the silver leaf of the lieutenant-colonel, and is enjoying the quiet life of a civilian.

But that fatal spirit of unrest from which I thought to escape, and which ruled my life for so many years, sometimes asserts its power, and at those times my thoughts turn back to the days when we were all lieutenants together, marching across the deserts and mountains of Arizona; back to my friends of the Eighth Infantry, that historic regiment, whose officers and men fought before the walls of Chapultepec and Mexico, back to my friends of the Sixth Cavalry, to the days at Camp MacDowell, where we slept under the stars, and watched the sun rise from behind the Four Peaks of the MacDowell Mountains: where we rode the big cavalry horses over the sands of the Maricopa desert, swung in our hammocks under the *ramadas*; swam in the red waters of the Verde River, ate canned peaches, pink butter and commissary hams, listened for the scratching of the centipedes as they scampered around the edges of our canvas-covered floors, found scorpions in our slippers, and rattlesnakes under our beds.

The old post is long since abandoned, but the Four Peaks still stand, wrapped in their black shadows by night, and their purple colours by day, waiting for the passing of the Apache and the coming of the white man, who shall dig his canals in those arid plains, and build his cities upon the ruins of the ancient Aztec dwellings.

The Sixth Cavalry, as well as the Eighth Infantry, has seen many vicissitudes since those days. Some of our gallant captains and lieutenants have won their stars, others have been slain in battle.

Dear, gentle Major Worth received wounds in the Cuban campaign, which caused his death, but he wore his stars before he obeyed the "last call."

The gay young officers of Angel Island days hold dignified commands in the Philippines, Cuba, and Alaska.

My early experiences were unusually rough. None of us seek such experiences, but possibly they bring with them a sort of recompense, in that simple comforts afterwards seem, by contrast, to be the greatest luxuries.

I am glad to have known the army: the soldiers, the line, and the Staff; it is good to think of honour and chivalry, obedience to duty and the pride of arms; to have lived amongst men whose motives were unselfish and whose aims were high; amongst men who served an ideal; who stood ready, at the call of their country, to give their lives for a Government which is, to them, the best in the world.

Sometimes I hear the still voices of the desert: they seem to be calling me through the echoes of the Past. I hear, in fancy, the wheels of the ambulance crunching the small broken stones of the *malapais*, or grating swiftly over the gravel of the smooth white roads of the river-bottoms. I hear the rattle of the ivory rings on the harness of the six-mule team; I see the soldiers marching on ahead; I see my white tent, so inviting after a long day's journey.

But how vain these fancies! Railroad and automobile have annihilated distance, the army life of those years is past and gone, and Arizona, as we knew it, has vanished from the face of the earth.

Appendix

Nantucket Island, June 1910.

When, a few years ago, I determined to write my recollections of life in the army, I was wholly unfamiliar with the methods of publishers, and the firm to whom I applied to bring out my book, did not urge upon me the advisability of having it electrotyped, firstly, because, as they said afterwards, I myself had such a very modest opinion of my book, and, secondly because they thought a book of so decidedly personal a character would not reach a sale of more than a few hundred copies at the farthest.

The matter of electrotyping was not even discussed between us. The entire edition of one thousand copies was exhausted in about a year, without having been carried on the lists of any bookseller or advertised in any way except through some circulars sent by myself to personal friends, and through several excellent reviews in prominent newspapers.

As the demand for the book continued, I have thought it advisable to re-issue it, adding a good deal that has come into my mind since its publication.

It was after the colonel's retirement that we came to spend the summers at Nantucket, and I began to enjoy the leisure that never comes into the life of an army woman during the active service of her husband. We were no longer expecting sudden orders, and I was able to think quietly over the events of the past.

My old letters which had been returned to me really gave me the inspiration to write the book and as I read them over, the people and the events therein described were recalled vividly to my mind—events which I had forgotten, people whom I had forgotten—events and people all crowded out of my memory for many years by the pressure of family cares, and the succession of changes in our stations, by anxiety during Indian campaigns, and the constant readjustment of my mind to new scenes and new friends.

And so, in the delicious quiet of the Autumn days at Nantucket, when the summer winds had ceased to blow and the frogs had ceased their pipings in the salt meadows, and the sea was wondering whether it should keep its summer blue or change into its winter grey, I sat down at my desk and began to write my story.

Looking out over the quiet ocean in those wonderful November days, when a peaceful calm brooded over all things, I gathered up all the threads of my various experiences and wove them together.

But the people and the lands I wrote about did not really exist for me; they were dream people and dream lands. I wrote of them as they had appeared to me in those early years, and, strange as it may seem, I did not once stop to think if the people and the lands still existed.

For a quarter of a century I had lived in the day that began with reveille and ended with "Taps."

Now on this enchanted island, there was no reveille to awaken us in the morning, and in the evening the only sound we could hear was the "ruck" of the waves on the far outer shores and the sad tolling of the bell buoy when the heaving swell of the ocean came rolling over the bar.

And so I wrote, and the story grew into a book which was published and sent out to friends and family.

As time passed on, I began to receive orders for the book from army officers, and then one day I received orders from people in Arizona and I awoke to the fact that Arizona was no longer the land of my memories. I began to receive booklets telling me of projected railroads, also pictures of wonderful buildings, all showing progress and prosperity.

And then came letters from some Presidents of railroads whose lines ran through Arizona, and from bankers and politicians and business men of Tucson, Phoenix and Yuma City. Photographs showing shady roads and streets, where once all was a glare and a sandy waste. Letters from mining men who knew every foot of the roads we had marched over; pictures of the great Laguna Dam on the Colorado, and of the quarters of the Government Reclamation Service Corps at Yuma.

These letters and pictures told me of the wonderful contrast presented by my story to the Arizona of today; and although I had not spared that country, in my desire to place before my children and friends a vivid picture of my life out there, all these men seemed willing to forgive me and even declared that my story might do as much to advance their interests and the prosperity of Arizona as anything which had been written with only that object in view.

My soul was calmed by these assurances, and I ceased to be distressed by thinking over the descriptions I had given of the unpleasant conditions existing in that country in the seventies.

In the meantime, the San Francisco Chronicle had published a good review of my book, and reproduced the photograph of Captain Jack Mellon, the noted pilot of the Colorado river, adding that he was undoubtedly one of the most picturesque characters who had ever lived on the Pacific Coast and that he had died some years ago.

And so he was really dead! And perhaps the others too, were all gone from the earth, I thought when one day I received a communication from an entire stranger, who informed me that the writer of the review in the San Francisco newspaper had been mistaken in the matter of Captain Mellon's death, that he had seen him recently and that he lived at San Diego. So I wrote to him and made haste to forward him a copy of my book, which reached him at Yuma, on the Colorado, and this is what he wrote:

Yuma, Dec. 15th, 1908.

My Dear Mrs. Summerhayes:

Your good book and letter came yesterday p. m., for which accept my thanks. My home is not in San Diego, but in Coronado, across the bay from San Diego. That is the reason I did not get your letter sooner.

In one hour after I received your book, I had orders for nine of them. All these books go to the official force of the Reclamation Service here who are damming the Colorado for the Government Irrigation Project. They are not Damming it as we formerly did, but with good solid masonry. The Dam is 4800 feet long and 300 feet wide and 10 feet above high water. In high water it will flow over the top of the Dam, but in low water the ditches or canals will take all the water out of the river, the approximate cost is three million. There will be a tunnel under the river at Yuma just below the bridge, to bring the water into Arizona which is thickly settled to the Mexican Line.

I have done nothing on the river since the 23rd of last August, at which date they closed the river to Navigation, and the only reason I am now in Yuma is trying to get something from Government for my boats made useless by the Dam. I expect to get a little, but not a tenth of what they cost me.

Your book could not have a better title: it is *Vanished Arizona* sure enough, vanished the good and warm Hearts that were here when you were. The people here now are cold blooded as a snake and are all trying to get the best of the other fellow.

There are but two alive that were on the river when you were on it. Polhemus and myself are all that are left, but I have many friends on this coast.

The nurse Patrocina died in Los Angeles last summer and the crying kid Jesusita she had on the boat when you went from Ehrenberg to the mouth of the river grew up to be the finest looking girl in these parts; She was the star witness in a murder trial in Los Angeles last winter, and her picture was in all of the papers.

I am sending you a picture of the Steamer *Mojave* which was not on the river when you were here. I made 20 trips with her up to the Virgin River, which is 145 miles above Fort Mojave, or 75 miles higher than any other man has gone with a boat: she was 10 feet longer than the *Gila* or any other boat ever on the river. (Excuse this blowing but it's the truth).

In 1864 I was on a trip down the Gulf of California, in a small sail boat and one of my companions was John Stanton. In Angel's Bay a man whom we were giving a passage to, murdered my partner and ran off with the boat and left Charley Ticen, John Stanton and myself on the beach. We were seventeen days tramping to a village with nothing to eat but cactus but I think I have told you the story before and what I want to know, is this Stanton alive. He belonged to New Bedford—his father had been master of a whale-ship.

When we reached Guaymas, Stanton found a friend, the mate of a steamer, the mate also belonged to New Bedford. When we parted, Stanton told me he was going home and was going to stay there, and as he was two years younger than me, he may still be in New Bedford, and as you are on the ground, maybe you can help me to find out.

All the people that I know praise your descriptive power and now my dear Mrs. Summerhayes I suppose you will have a hard time wading through my scrawl but I know you will be generous and remember that I went to sea when a little over nine years of age and had my pen been half as often in my hand as a marlin spike, I would now be able to write a much clearer hand.

I have a little bungalow on Coronado Beach, across the bay from San Diego, and if you ever come there, you or your husband, you are welcome; while I have a bean you can have half. I would like to see you and talk over old times. Yuma is quite a place now; no more adobes built; it is brick and concrete, cement sidewalks and flower gardens with electric light and a good water system.

My home is within five minutes walk of the Pacific Ocean. I was born at Digby, Nova Scotia, and the first music I ever heard was the surf of the Bay of Fundy, and when I close my eyes forever I hope the surf of the Pacific will be the last sound that will greet my ears.

I read Vanished Arizona last night until after midnight, and thought what we both had gone through since you first came up the Colorado with me. My acquaintance with the army was always pleasant, and like Tom Moore I often say:

Let fate do her worst, there are relics of joy bright dreams of the past which she cannot destroy! Which come in the night-time of sorrow and care And bring back the features that joy used to wear. Long, long be my heart with such memories filled!

I suppose the colonel goes down to the Ship Chandler's and gams with the old whaling captains. When I was a boy, there was a wealthy family of ship-owners in New Bedford by the name of Robinson. I saw one of their ships in Bombay, India, that was in 1854, her name was the Mary Robinson, and altho' there were over a hundred ships on the bay, she was the handsomest there.

Well, good friend, I am afraid I will tire you out, so I will belay this, and with best wishes for you and yours,

I am, yours truly,

J. A. Mellon.

P. S.—Fisher is long since called to his Long Home.

I had fancied, when *Vanished Arizona* was published, that it might possibly appeal to the sympathies of women, and that men would lay it aside as a sort of a "woman's book"—but I have received more really sympathetic letters from men than I have from women, all telling me, in different words, that the human side of the story had appealed to them, and I suppose this comes from the fact that originally I wrote it for my children, and felt perfect freedom to put my whole self into it. And now that the book is entirely out of my hands, I am glad that I wrote it as I did, for if I had stopped to think that my dream people might be real people, and that the real people would read it, I might never have had the courage to write it at all.

The many letters I have received of which there have been several hundred I am sure, have been so interesting that I reproduce a few more of them here:

Fort Benjamin Harrison,
Indianapolis, Indiana.
January 10, 1909.

My dear Mrs. Summerhayes:

I have just read the book. It is a good book, a true book, one of the best kind of books. After taking it up I did not lay it down till it was finished—till with you I had again gone over the *malapais* deserts of Arizona, and recalled my own meetings with you at Niobrara and at old Fort Marcy or Santa Fe. You were my *cicerone* in the old town and I couldn't have had a better one—or more charming one.

The book has recalled many memories to me. Scarcely a name you mention but is or was a friend. Major Van Vliet loaned me his copy, but I shall get one of my own and shall tell my friends in the East that, if they desire a true picture of army life as it appears to the army woman, they must read your book.

For my part I feel that I must congratulate you on your successful work and thank you for the pleasure you have given me in its perusal.

With cordial regard to you and yours, and with best wishes for many happy years.

Very sincerely yours,
L. W. V. Kennon, Maj. 10th Inf.

Headquarters Third Brigade,
National Guard of Pennsylvania,
Wilkes-Barre, Pennsylvania.
January 19, 1908.
Dear Madam:
I am sending you herewith my check for two copies of
Vanished Arizona. This summer our mutual friend, Colonel Beaumont (late 4th U. S. Cav.) ordered two copies for
me and I have given them both away to friends whom I
wanted to have read your delightful and charming book. I
am now ordering one of these for another friend and wish
to keep one in my record library as a memorable story of
the bravery and courage of the noble band of army men
and women who helped to blaze the pathway of the nation's progress in its course of Empire Westward.
No personal record written, which I have read, tells so
splendidly of what the good women of our army endured
in the trials that beset the army in the life on the plains in
the days succeeding the Civil War. And all this at a time
when the nation and its people were caring but little for
you all and the struggles you were making.
I will be pleased indeed if you will kindly inscribe your
name in one of the books you will send me.
    Sincerely Yours,   C. B. Dougherty,
                         Brig. Gen'l N. G. Pa.
Jan. 19, 1908

Schenectady, N. Y.
June 8th, 1908.
Mrs. John W. Summerhayes,
    North Shore Hill, Nantucket, Mass.
My Dear Mrs. Summerhayes:
Were I to say that I enjoyed *Vanished Arizona*, I should
very inadequately express my feelings about it, because
there is so much to arouse emotions deeper than what we
call "enjoyment;" it stirs the sympathies and excites our
admiration for your courage and your fortitude. In a word,

the story, honest and unaffected, yet vivid, has in it that touch of nature which makes kin of us all.

How actual knowledge and experience broadens our minds! Your appreciation of, and charity for, the weaknesses of those living a lonely life of deprivation on the frontier, impressed me very much. I wish too, that what you say about the canteen could be published in every newspaper in America.

Very sincerely yours,

M. F. Westover,

Secretary Gen'l Electric Co.

The Military Service Institution

of the United States.

Governor's Island, N.Y.

June 25, 1908.

Dear Mrs. Summerhayes:

I offer my personal congratulations upon your success in producing a work of such absorbing interest to all friends of the army, and so instructive to the public at large.

I have just finished reading the book, from cover to cover, to my wife and we have enjoyed it thoroughly.

Will you please advise me where the book can be purchased in New York, or otherwise mail two copies to me at 203 W. 54th Street, New York City, with memo of price per copy, that I may remit the amount.

Very truly yours,

T. F. Rodenbough,

Secretary and Editor (Brig. Gen'l. U. S. A.)

Yale University, New Haven, Conn.

May 15, 1910.

Dear Mrs. Summerhayes:

I have read every word of your book *Vanished Arizona* with intense interest. You have given a vivid account of what you actually saw and lived through, and nobody can resist the truthfulness and reality of your narrative. The book is a real contribution to American history, and to the chronicles of army life.

Faithfully yours,   Wm. Lyon Phelps,
[Professor of English literature at Yale University.]

Lonaconing, MD., Jan. 2, 1909.
Col. J. W. Summerhays,
New Rochelle, N. Y.

Dear Sir:

Captain William Baird, 6th Cavalry, retired, now at Annapolis, sent me Mrs. Summerhay's book to read, and I have read it with delight, for I was in "K" when Mrs. Summerhays "took on" in the 8th. Myself and my brother, Michael, served in "K" Company from David's Island to Camp Apache. Doubtless you have forgotten me, but I am sure that you remember the tall fifer of "K", Michael Gurnett. He was killed at Camp Mohave in Sept. 1885, while in Company "G" of the 1st Infantry. I was five years in "K", but my brother re-enlisted in "K", and afterward joined the First. He served in the 31st, 22nd, 8th and 1st. Oh, that little book!

We're all in it, even poor Charley Bowen. Mrs. Summerhays should have written a longer story. She soldiered long enough with the 8th in the "bloody 70's" to be able to write a book five times as big. For what she's done, God bless her! She is entitled to the Irishman's benediction: "May every hair in her head be a candle to light her soul to glory." We poor old Regulars have little said about us in print, and wish to God that *Vanished Arizona* was in the hands of every old veteran of the "Marching 8th."

If I had the means I would send a copy to our 1st Serg't Bernard Moran, and the other old comrades at the Soldiers' Home. But, alas, evil times have fallen upon us, and—I'm not writing a *jeremiad*—I took the book from the post office and when I saw the crossed guns and the "8" there was a lump in my throat, and I went into the barber shop and read it through before I left. A friend of mine was in the shop and when I came to Pringle's death, he said, "Gurnett, that must be a sad book you're reading, why man, you're crying."

I believe I was, but they were tears of joy. And, Oh, Lord, to think of Bowen having a full page in history; but, after all, maybe he deserved it. And that picture of my company commander! [Worth]. Long, long, have I gazed on it. I was only sixteen and a half years old when I joined his company at David's Island, Dec. 6th, 1871. Folliot A. Whitney was 1st lieutenant and Cyrus Earnest, 2nd. What a fine man Whitney was. A finer man nor truer gentleman ever wore a shoulder strap. If he had been company commander I'd have re-enlisted and stayed with him. I was always afraid of Worth, though he was always good to my brother and myself. I deeply regretted Lieutenant Whitney's death in Cuba, and I watched Major Worth's career in the last war. It nearly broke my heart that I could not go. Oh, the rattle of the war drum and the bugle calls and the marching troops, it set me crazy, and me not able to take a hand in the scrap.

Mrs. Summerhays calls him Wm. T. Worth, isn't it Wm. S. Worth?

The copy I have read was loaned me by Captain Baird; he says it's a Christmas gift from General Carter, and I must return it. My poor wife has read it with keen interest and says she: "William, I am going to have that book for my children," and she'll get it, yea, verily! she will.

Well, Colonel, I'm right glad to know that you are still on this side of the great divide, and I know that you and Mrs. S. will be glad to hear from an old "walk-a-heap" of the 8th.

I am working for a Cumberland newspaper—Lonaconing reporter—and I will send you a copy or two of the paper with this. And now, permit me to subscribe myself your

Comrade In Arms,

William A. Gurnett.

Dear Mrs. Summerhayes:

Read your book—in fact when I got started I forgot my bedtime (and you know how rigid that is) and sat it through.

It has a bully note of the old army—it was all worthwhile—they had colour, those days.

I say—now suppose you had married a man who kept a drug store—see what you would have had and see what you would have missed.

Yours,   Frederic Remington.

CPSIA information can be obtained
at www.ICGtesting.com
Printed in the USA
LVHW091315230221
679737LV00014B/55/J